IMPLEMENTATION STRATEGIES FOR ENVIRONMENTAL TAXES

ORGANISATION FOR ECONOMIC CO-OPERATION AND DEVELOPMENT

ORGANISATION FOR ECONOMIC CO-OPERATION AND DEVELOPMENT

Pursuant to Article 1 of the Convention signed in Paris on 14th December 1960, and which came into force on 30th September 1961, the Organisation for Economic Co-operation and Development (OECD) shall promote policies designed:

— to achieve the highest sustainable economic growth and employment and a rising standard of living in Member countries, while maintaining financial stability, and thus to contribute to the development of the world economy;

— to contribute to sound economic expansion in Member as well as non-member countries in the process of economic development; and

— to contribute to the expansion of world trade on a multilateral, non-discriminatory basis in accordance with international obligations.

The original Member countries of the OECD are Austria, Belgium, Canada, Denmark, France, Germany, Greece, Iceland, Ireland, Italy, Luxembourg, the Netherlands, Norway, Portugal, Spain, Sweden, Switzerland, Turkey, the United Kingdom and the United States. The following countries became Members subsequently through accession at the dates indicated hereafter: Japan (28th April 1964), Finland (28th January 1969), Australia (7th June 1971), New Zealand (29th May 1973) and Mexico (18th May 1994). The Commission of the European Communities takes part in the work of the OECD (Article 13 of the OECD Convention).

Publié en français sous le titre :

STRATÉGIES DE MISE EN ŒUVRE DES ÉCOTAXES

FOREWORD

The role of economic instruments, in particular ecotaxes, in environmental policy, significantly developed in OECD countries over the last decade. In the case of ecotaxes, it is important to ensure an effective integration, in fact a complementarity, between fiscal and environmental policies. The need for such complementarity has been clearly recognised by the OECD Committee on Fiscal Affairs and the Environment Policy Committee, stating, in their 1993 study* that "environmental and fiscal policies can and should be made mutually reinforcing". This is why it was decided to carry out an in depth analysis of the various implementation aspects and constraints of environmental taxes, as well as their fiscal and economic implications. This work was done under the supervision of a joint group of fiscal and environmental government experts.

The Secretariat thanks the members of the Joint Sessions on Taxation and Environment for their input and Ms Béatrice Fournier, consultant, for her contribution to the preparation of the report.

This report has been approved by the Committee on Fiscal affairs and the Environment Policy Committee. The OECD Council agreed to the derestriction of the report **on 11 January 1996.**

---

* *Taxation and the Environment: Complementary Policies,* OECD, 1993.

TABLE OF CONTENTS

Executive summary 7

Chapter 1
CONTEXT AND SCOPE OF THE STUDY

1.1. Background and objectives 9
1.2. Main characteristics and trends in OECD countries 9
1.3. Basic concepts of environmental taxation 10
1.4. Environmental taxation and regulation 11
1.5. Regulation and tax policy integration 13
1.6. Scope of the report 14

Notes 14

Annex to Chapter 1
Table A.1. Overview of environmentally-related taxes and charges in OECD countries 16
References 18

Chapter 2
DESIGNING AND IMPLEMENTING ENVIRONMENTAL TAXES

2.1. Background 19
2.2. Developing an appropriate policy framework 19
    Linkage 20
    Acceptability 21
2.3. Designing environmental taxes 22
    The tax base and the point of imposition 22
    How to determine the tax rate? 23
2.4. Administrative and compliance issues 26
    Regulatory authorities 26
    Monitoring 28
    Administrative and compliance costs 28
2.5. ''Tax Packaging'' issues 28
    Elimination of non-price barriers 29
    Revenue recycling 29
    Distributional effects and compensation measures 31
2.6. Concluding remarks 32

Notes 32
References 33

Chapter 3
INTERNATIONAL IMPLICATIONS OF ENVIRONMENTAL TAXES

3.1. Introduction 35
3.2. Trade and environmental taxes 35
    Environmental taxes and competitiveness: key factors 36
    Short-term versus long-term effects 37
3.3. Trade: key factors and assumptions 37
3.4. Empirical evidence 40
    Effects on competitiveness and trade 40
    Environmental effectiveness and leakage issues 42

3.5. Mitigation measures 43
      Sectoral differentiation of environmental taxes 43
      Border tax adjustments 44
      Implementation strategy of environmental taxes 45
3.6. Conclusions 45

Notes 46
References 47

Chapter 4
DISTRIBUTIONAL EFFECTS OF ENVIRONMENTAL TAXES AND COMPENSATION MEASURES

4.1. Introduction 49
4.2. Analytical framework 49
      Relevant costs and benefits 49
      Formal and effective incidence 50
      The baseline for comparison 50
      Relevant distributional dimensions 50
4.3. Empirical evidence and simulation results 51
      Distributional impacts of carbon taxes and other energy taxes 51
      Distributional implications of other taxes 55
4.4. Policy implications 56
      Mitigation and compensation 57
      Compensation through adjustments to other taxes 58
      Other compensation approaches 59
      The role of adjustment policies 60
4.5. Conclusions 61

Notes 62
References 63

Chapter 5
THE USE OF REVENUES FROM ENVIRONMENTAL TAXES

5.1. Alternative uses of revenues 65
5.2. The incidence of an environmental tax 66
5.3. Taxes on energy resource owners 66
      A consumption based energy tax 66
      A production based energy tax 67
      Tax exemptions for energy intensive sectors 68
      The sustainability of energy tax revenues 68
      The impact on employment 68
5.4. Environmental taxes and complementary policies 68
      Taxes on labour 68
      Labour taxation, real wages and employment 69
      Taxes on capital 69
      Empirical evidence 70
5.5. Conclusions 71

Notes 71
References 72

Chapter 6
SUMMARY AND CONCLUSIONS

6.1. A new trend in environmental policy 73
6.2. Designing and implementing environmental taxes 73
6.3. International implications of environmental taxes 76
6.4. Distributive effects of environmental taxes and compensation measures 79
6.5. The use of environmental tax revenues 80

Annexes 83

A.1. Environmental taxation of energy 85
A.2. Environmental taxes in energy sectors 89

EXECUTIVE SUMMARY

Environmental taxes and other economic instruments became popular with policy makers in the early 1980s, as their potential for achieving environmental goals and maintaining economic efficiency was recognised. While many environmental taxes were introduced in OECD Member countries, there are still few examples of comprehensive "ecological" tax reforms. This report analyses the issues that arise before and during the introduction of environmental taxes and draws on the experiences of Member countries implementing them. It builds on earlier OECD work on this area.*

After a brief overview of recent trends in OECD countries, Chapter 1 reviews basic concepts and definitions of environmental taxation. It then discusses the attractiveness of environmental taxes to policy makers, particularly in comparison with command and control measures. A greater use of market mechanisms can be expected to achieve greater environmental effectiveness and economic efficiency. Environmental tax instruments should be part of an integrated policy, where both environmental taxation and regulation have a complementary role to play.

Chapter 2 addresses a number of design issues – such as how to determine the appropriate tax base and tax rate – and considers a number of administrative and compliance questions. Environmental taxes ideally should be imposed as close as possible to the point of emission. Given the authorities are unlikely to have all the necessary information to determine the appropriate tax rate or even the tax base, these may need to be revised in the light of experience. But the need for change should be weighed against the benefits of a stable and predictable tax system for business planning. Advance notification and gradual implementation allow a better assessment of the appropriate rate and help avoid unnecessary economic costs from disrupting investment plans. The question of "tax packaging" is approached by first considering what can be done to reduce non-price barriers – such as lack of information and technology transfer – and then the use of tax revenues. Given the risk that related expenditures may short-circuit normal processes of programme evaluation and create rigidities

in the allocation of spending, it is generally accepted that, under most circumstances, earmarking revenues to a particular spending programme should be avoided.

Chapter 3 provides a comprehensive overview of the mechanisms by which ecotaxes can affect trade. It looks both at the microeconomic level – where some sectors or firms may be more adversely affected than others – and the macroeconomic level, where trade balances and trade patterns may change. The factors that may determine the impact of ecotaxes on competitiveness and trade flows are reviewed. The chapter then considers issues of "leakage" and policy effectiveness: the potential relocation of production to other countries with no, or less stringent, environmental policies. The potential for mitigation and compensation measures to alleviate the impact of environmental taxes on domestic industry and for positive impacts on competitiveness by encouraging technological innovation is considered. Ecotax revenues can be used to help reduce their impact on competitiveness and trade, but some offsetting measures may be necessary in the short- and medium-term, at least for some firms or sectors. The mitigation measures need to preserve the incentive effects of the environmental tax and maintain transparency under international trade agreements. Border tax adjustments may help reduce the effect on competitiveness, but their use may not always be indicated particularly when pollution arises from production processes and methods, either for reasons of environmental effectiveness or non-compliance with international trade rules, or because of their impracticability. Many of the negative impacts of environmental taxes on trade and competitiveness can be avoided by early announcement and gradual implementation.

Chapter 4 focuses on the distributional effects of environmental taxes. It does not attempt a complete review of the numerous empirical studies, but assesses how compensation schemes can reduce the burden on those most affected by the tax while preserving the cost-saving potential of the tax instrument. Distributional impacts differ depending on the degree of necessity of the activities or products subject to the tax and the availability of substitutes.

Chapter 5 explores how environmental tax revenues could be used to promote growth and employment. Some revenues would be necessary to alleviate the impact on trade and competitiveness and on the groups most affected by the tax, as discussed in the previous chapters on trade and distributional issues. The chapter examines

---

* See *Taxation and the Environment: Complementary Policies*, OECD, Paris, 1993; and *Environmental Taxes in OECD Countries*, OECD, Paris, 1995.

how the revenues from the ecotax could be used to reduce the overall tax burden on labour or other factors of production, compensating for the potential loss in employment created by the ecotax. The best use of environmental tax revenues will depend on the economic and fiscal circumstances in each country.

The final chapter draws a number of conclusions from the preceding discussion. It summarises a number of policy options open to governments implementing environmental taxes, and reviews the international implications, the distributional impacts and employment effects.

Chapter 1

CONTEXT AND SCOPE OF THE STUDY

1.1. Background and objectives

At their meeting at OECD in January 1991, Environment Ministers "called upon the OECD to examine possibilities for adapting taxation systems to achieve both socioeconomic and environmental objectives without excessive administrative complexity". The Committee on Fiscal Affairs (CFA) of the OECD also decided at its meeting in January 1991 that work on taxation and the environment should be given a high priority in the Committee's work program. As a result, a joint task force on Taxation and Environment was created by the Environment Policy Committee and the Committee on Fiscal Affairs to identify, review and analyse the issues raised by economic instruments such as taxes and charges, and the possible environmental consequences of fiscal policies. This task force completed its work in October 1992 [see OECD (1993a)]. One of its main conclusions is that fiscal and environmental policies can and should be made mutually reinforcing. It also raised the need to study the implementation of environmental taxes in greater depth, both at national and international levels. This led to the organisation of Joint Sessions on Taxation and Environment, combining environmental and fiscal experts. The work programme of the Joint Sessions covers: i) implementation issues relating to environmental taxes; ii) the trade implications of environmental taxes; iii) the distributional impacts of environmental taxes; and iv) the use of revenues and employment issues relating to environmental taxes.

The aim of this report is to present a set of practical recommendations to help countries develop implementation strategies that will realise the full potential of environmental taxes and their acceptability as environmental policy instruments. After a review of the issues related to the design and implementation of environmental taxes, the report focuses on three inter-related issues and the policy options: trade and competitiveness, the distributional effects and alternative uses of ecotax revenues. While many of these issues were raised in the previous report on taxation and environment (cited above), this report covers them in greater detail, and as such is self-contained.

1.2. Main characteristics and trends in OECD countries

The first OECD survey of environmental taxes [see OECD (1993c)], based on 1990-91 data, reported a number of explicit and implicit charges and taxes, which were either implemented with a specific environmental objective, or, while introduced for non-environmental reasons, are now designed to reflect environmental considerations. A number of taxes on energy and on motor vehicles were surveyed, including consumption and value-added taxes. More significantly, the survey covered the carbon taxes implemented in four OECD Member countries: Finland, the Netherlands, Norway and Sweden. Taxes on other goods included taxes on batteries, plastic carrier bags, drinks sold in disposable containers, pesticides, tires, CFCs and halons. Water charges, waste disposal and management charges, and taxes and charges on noise pollution were also reported, along with some environmentally related provisions in income tax systems.

A new survey has been conducted for 1993-94 [see Table A.1 in the annex to this chapter for an overview of the current use of environmental taxes and the *Survey of Environmental Taxes in OECD Countries* (OECD, 1995) for a more detailed description]. Many existing taxes have been redesigned to reflect better their environmental purpose, and more goods are taxed for environmental purposes. The main trends in environmental taxation fall into two broad categories. One group of countries has radically restructured the tax system. It is argued that a shift in the tax burden away from income towards consumption taxes, including environmental taxes, may reduce structural problems in the economy. Explicit environmental considerations tend to play a growing role in the design of tax reforms. Arguments to this effect were, for example, among the reasons for the Danish tax reform in 1993. The Danish government's proposals stressed the need to shift taxation away from wage income and on to consumption and production which have a negative effect on the environment. A similar set of policy objectives form the basis of the changes in tax systems in Finland, Norway, the Netherlands and Sweden. In these cases, the restructuring is mainly confined to energy taxes. A discussion of the tax burden on energy products resulting from those tax reforms is presented at the end of the report, as well as an overview of the structure and administration of carbon/energy taxes in Denmark, Finland, the Netherlands, Norway and Sweden.

A second category consists of countries that use environmental taxes on a smaller scale than the first, for example, Austria, Germany, Belgium, France and Switzerland. There has also been increased use of environmental taxes in these countries – of both new and existing taxes – but within a narrower framework than a comprehensive tax reform. There also appears to be a trend towards stressing the incentive effects of environmental taxes. Existing taxes, for instance on energy, are being restructured to provide a greater incentive to reduce emissions. Considerable benefits may accrue from simply increasing the rate of existing energy taxes. The United Kingdom is now committed to a yearly 5 per cent real duty increase on road fuels.

1.3. Basic concepts of environmental taxation

The aim of environmental tax instruments is to improve the environment by pricing its various uses. In the case of pollution, the purpose of tax instruments is to reduce the level of harmful emissions generated by production processes or consumption, by adjusting relative prices and changing market signals to discourage particular consumption patterns or production methods and to encourage the use of alternatives that lead to less environment degradation. Environmental tax instruments include specific taxes and charges, tax allowances, and tax differentials between products where the most environmentally friendly product is taxed least (see Box 1.1 for definitions). For convenience, these tax measures are referred to as "ecotaxes" or "environmental taxes", although these are not legal terms. Given the more widespread use of tax instruments to reduce pollution, the report refers in most cases to pollution related taxes.

Box 1.1. DEFINITIONS OF ENVIRONMENTAL TAX INSTRUMENTS

Emission taxes involve tax payments that are directly related to the measurement (or estimation) of the pollution caused, whether emitted into air, water or on the soil, or due to the generation of noise. Emission taxes generally deal with one type of emission at a time. They are directed to the last link in the chain, that is, to those actually emitting a certain substance into the environment, and are usually only suitable for stationary sources because of their high monitoring and administrative costs.

Product charges or taxes can be a substitute for emission taxes when direct measurement of emissions is not possible. More generally, product taxes may be levied to price environmental effects correctly, and could be used to correct externalities other than pollution. A product tax may be levied on the units of harmful substance contained in products: for instance, a carbon tax is based on the carbon content of each particular fossil fuel. The product tax may also be levied per unit of the product, if the objective is to reduce usage of the product generally. Product charges may be applied to raw materials, intermediate, or final (consumer) products. When applied to consumer products, they are often called **consumption taxes** or final-product taxes. Consumption taxes may be used when pollution is closely linked to consumer demand, such as disposable products that compete with reusable alternatives, or non-fuel efficient cars. In this case, the taxation may be linked to the product itself or part of its contents that are detrimental to the environment. When applied to raw material (e.g. coal to produce electricity) or intermediate products (e.g. polyvinylchloride to produce plastic), product taxes are referred to as **input taxes**. Emission taxes on production activities and input taxes are referred to as **production taxes**.

Tax differentiation relates to variations in existing indirect taxes, such as excise duties, sales taxes, or value added taxes for environmental ends. Goods and services that are associated with environmental damage in production and consumption may be taxed more heavily (e.g. most OECD countries apply different excise tax rates to leaded and unleaded petrol).

User Charges are payments related to the service delivered. Only those connected to the relevant public service are charged. The revenues raised are used to provide a service, such as the collection and public treatment of effluents. They are considered environmental tax instruments because the service they fund seeks to improve the quality of the environment and to reduce the use of natural resources such as water and land. Given their cost recovery nature, user charges are a direct application of the polluter-pays-principle.

Tax reliefs consist of various provisions in income tax systems designed to encourage some kind of behaviour, either by consumers or businesses. The most common form of tax relief is accelerated depreciation, but many countries also provide investment tax credits for certain types of investment, such as pollution control equipment, or for research and development.

In theory, environmental taxes force producers and consumers to consider the cost of pollution or other externalities in their economic decisions. Producers and consumers may switch to less polluting products or alternatives if the tax rate is high enough. In the case of emissions taxes, if firms are to be taxed at $1 000 for each tonne of pollution emitted, and if it costs firm A only $500 to reduce pollution by one tonne, then it would make economic sense for firm A to spend the $500 for pollution abatement and avoid paying the $1 000. Firm A has an incentive to reduce pollution up to the point where the marginal abatement cost is equal to the tax rate. If the cost of reducing pollution by another tonne is higher than $1 000 for other firms, then those firms would rather pay the tax. The incentive effect of emission taxes leads firms to reduce pollution to different degrees: firms with high abatement costs will reduce pollution less than others and pay more taxes.

Most environmental taxes are not truly "Pigouvian" taxes, as they are not based directly on the units of emissions and the associated level of environmental damage. A Pigouvian tax is a specific tax imposed at a rate where there would not be any additional net benefit gained by reducing emissions by another unit. To evaluate the level of the tax properly requires an estimate of the extra benefit from reducing one unit of pollution and the cost of a reduction in emissions. This information is rarely available. Because of the high cost of measuring pollutants and of enforcement, the taxation of commodities may be preferred to taxation of emissions themselves. As it would be too expensive to determine the socially optimal level of emissions as in a Pigouvian tax, the tax rate is usually set on either emissions or on products to obtain an acceptable level of environmental improvement. This level of emissions may be changed over time as new information becomes available to the public and the government. While there may be uncertainty about the level of pollution reduction to be achieved, there will still be improvement in the environment. Here, uncertainty is only positively harmful if it is the direction of the effect which is uncertain, not the extent of the effect.

Taxes imposed on products rather than on emissions themselves may not be efficient if there does not exist a *direct* and *stable* link between the goods and the damaging emissions. In the case of global warming, the taxation of carbon emissions indirectly through a product tax on fossil fuels is efficient since carbon is emitted in fixed proportion to the amount of each fossil fuel burned, and there is no end-of-pipe technology that leads to a change in the relationship between the fuels and the carbon emitted and the environmental damage. However, the relationship between the environmental problem, the level of emissions and the taxed product is often not stable. For instance, two power stations may produce the same output and use the same level of fuels, but the polluting emissions will differ if one of them uses end-of-pipe desulphurisation technology. The deterioration of local air quality, although linked to the burning of fuels, would not necessarily be solved by the taxation of fuels alone, as there is no fixed relationship between the use of fuels and the quality of air. Local air quality depends on atmospheric conditions, the time of day and the maintenance of vehicles as well as the use of fuels. In this case, the taxation of fuels needs to be accompanied by regulatory instruments, since taxation alone cannot deliver the appropriate air quality. The efficiency of an environmental taxes is dependent on a close relationship between the taxed products and their detrimental emissions.

Environmental tax reliefs, such as incentives to invest in pollution abatement equipment through accelerated depreciation rates or investment tax credits, may lead to an inefficient level of pollution abatement or to over-investment in one form of technology. In addition, even if each firm has an incentive to reduce pollution, the implicit subsidy created by the tax provision may prevent the exit of firms from the industry and reduce the effectiveness of the tax provision.[1] Moreover, the use of tax preferences for environmental purposes may be in conflict with the OECD Polluter-Pays-Principle and with recent tax reforms which eliminated tax preferences to broaden the tax base and reduce tax rates.

1.4. Environmental taxation and regulation

Recent OECD work [see OECD (1989), (1991), (1993a), (1994a)] identified advantages to greater use of market mechanisms in environmental policy, compared with a command and control approach based on environmental regulations. In some situations the application of tax instruments may not be warranted, and in others environmental regulations may be difficult or impossible to implement. Any comparison of cost efficiency and environmental effectiveness between tax instruments and regulation is limited to situations where both policy instruments could realistically be applied.

Ecotaxes change relative prices to ensure that polluters take account of the effects of their activities on the environment. Compared with command and control measures, ecotaxes are more flexible: polluters are free to adapt to market signals in the most cost effective manner. Polluters have at least three options to reduce emissions besides reducing output. They may install pollution abatement technology, improve production efficiency or change processes to reduce the use of polluting substances. When taxes are imposed only on inputs, producers cannot reduce their tax payments by using place end-of-pipe technology. If fixed at an appropriate level, environmental taxes minimise the overall cost of achieving a given pollution control target, even though some firms or industries may face higher costs with ecotaxes than with regulation. This is often referred to as "static efficiency". Tax instruments are self-regulating, since once in place, market forces tend to do the rest. Lower administrative, monitoring and enforcement costs may result. Hence taxation is an efficient regulatory instrument.

Because polluters have to pay taxes on emissions, ecotaxes provide a permanent incentive to reduce pollution and to innovate [see OECD (1993*a*)]. This is known as ''dynamic efficiency'': the tax provides a continuing incentive to innovate in order to reduce pollution even below target levels to reduce tax payments. The counterargument is that the burden of the tax leaves firms with fewer resources for research and development, and that the creation of innovative, less polluting methods of production may be slower than under regulation. Nevertheless, in a competitive market, especially in a fast growing industry, market forces should push industry to further innovation and to lowering emissions and tax payments. This dynamic efficiency is not necessarily limited to tax instruments. While it is true that environmental policies based on command and control measures are often associated with a prescribed set of technologies that lead to undesirable rigidities, environmental regulations based on ''best available technology'' may also present some dynamic efficiency. Moreover, environmental taxes may not always provide the same dynamic feature in areas of innovation. For instance, an input tax may not provide an incentive to install available emission reduction technologies such as scrubbers; and a consumption tax may not provide incentives to producers to reduce emissions.

In addition to being potentially more cost efficient and environmentally effective than command and control measures, environmental taxes also raise revenues that would not arise with regulations. Some of the revenues may be used to pay for the costs of administration and enforcement of the tax. In the case of regulation, the administrative costs may often be higher than for ecotaxes, and the government has to cover those costs by raising revenues from other, distortionary taxes. There is a number of options for the use of ecotax revenues: deficit reduction, expenditure programmes – environmental or other – and reduction of other taxes. Each of

these alternatives should be judged on its own merits and in relation to a set of criteria including employment impacts (see Chapter 5). Taxes – often accompanied by regulations – may lead to large reductions or the complete elimination of emissions over time. Governments must take account of the diminishing tax revenues in their fiscal planning.

Another potential benefit of environmental taxes and charges relative to regulation featured in the Task Force report [OECD (1993*a*)] is that a policy based on market instruments may be less vulnerable to ''regulatory capture'', whereby regulators may get too close to the industry they supervise. Regulatory policies are often based on firm-by-firm negotiation. However, regulatory capture may also occur with taxation. In addition, the net tax burden of firms may not be particularly transparent, given the tax deductions or exemptions allowed in the general tax system. Nevertheless, tax instruments are generally seen to be more transparent than regulations.

While there may be important differences between environmental taxes and command and control measures, there are also some similarities. Both taxes and regulations may affect production costs, employment and the competitive position of domestic firms. Both may have distributional impacts that necessitate compensatory measures. Effective monitoring and policing to identify violations is required to enforce both policies, along with a framework of administrative and legal processes and a set of penalties. Both have to be implemented in a world with imperfect information, imperfect competition, market regulations and other government policies.

While environmental taxes have a number of advantages over command and control measures, regulation still has an important role in environmental policy. Taxes may not be appropriate in some cases, such as highly toxic substances where a complete ban is necessary. With suitable monitoring and enforcement, regulation provides

---

Box 1.2. **FISCAL AND ECONOMIC EFFICIENCY**

Efficiency in a fiscal sense is when a tax raises revenues with as little impact as possible on production or consumption patterns. Efficiency in environmental terms refers to a policy that induces agents to change their behaviour with the least economic costs, in order to meet environmental goals.

In fiscal terms, an efficient tax system is one that raises the target revenues with the minimum market distortions. An efficient tax system should raise the necessary revenues while having as little effect as possible on the allocation of resources and create as little excess burden or deadweight loss as possible. However, this assumes that markets work perfectly (where all costs and benefits are internalised), leading to an efficient allocation of resources. Existing taxes on consumption, income and labour are said to be inefficient in a fiscal sense since they distort market signals (relative prices).

Environmental taxes help change relative prices and provide incentives to use more environment-friendly products and methods of production. By pricing the environment and thereby reducing market distortions, environmental taxes not only reduce externalities, but they also improve economic efficiency.

a greater degree of "certainty" about the policy outcome in environmental effectiveness, particularly when persistent and toxic substances are concerned. Regulation is more direct than tax instruments which induce behavioural change through the price mechanism. Both instruments have a role in environmental policy, and each should be analysed and implemented so as to ensure the most efficient reduction in environmental damage.

Environmental taxes have to take account of equity considerations as well as efficiency. Environmental taxes impose an additional burden on industries and consumers, as with any tax, which may lead to lower output and lower employment, even after ecotax revenues have been redistributed. This may be more than compensated at the margin by an improved quality of the environment, enhancing the welfare of the group which suffered from environmental deterioration. Those who benefit from an improved environment are not necessarily those facing increased costs due to ecotaxes, but those who privately benefit from environmental damage – the polluters –, and those paying the tax. However, some means of compensation may be necessary to make the environmental tax more acceptable and equitable.

Environmental taxes have to be implemented alongside the existing regulations and tax system. In most cases, environmental taxes are introduced in combination with other instruments, for example with command and control measures in so-called "mixed systems". Environmental taxes may be part of an agreement with industry whereby firms that "voluntarily" agree to meet certain environmental targets will not have to pay taxes on the remaining emissions for some years (e.g. in waste management). There may be other related externalities that also require consideration. Environmental taxation may be part of a package of measures to help move towards "sustainable consumption".

Implementation strategies for environmental taxes will differ when pollution arises from either consumption or production, or both, when their use is more common and their rationale familiar to the public, and when many trading partners implement the tax at the same time. All these factors that set the stage will need careful consideration for a successful implementation of environmental taxes.

1.5. Regulation and tax policy integration

At their meeting in January 1991, OECD Environment Ministers "called for improved policy integration in *all economic sectors*. Ministers underlined the need for governments to identify and eliminate those subsidies, taxes or other market interventions that distort the use of environmental resources, thereby impacting adversely on environmental policy objectives."

Current tax provisions may be detrimental to the environment by indirectly encouraging activities that lead to externalities.[2] Many of these measures were introduced for industrial or social reasons that may still be valid. However, given new scientific evidence and a deteriorating environment, the environmental costs of these provisions may now outweigh other benefits. A review of current tax systems in the light of environmental concerns may be necessary. Before introducing new environmental taxes, governments may wish to consider modifying or eliminating current tax provisions that encourage polluting activities. This could be part of a general tax reform designed to eliminate tax preferences, enlarge the tax base, and so allow lower tax rates. Table 1.1 gives examples of current tax provisions that can have an adverse environmental impact. There are many examples, particularly in the transport, energy and agriculture sectors [see OECD (1992), and Barde and Button].

Other government policies besides taxation, such as subsidies or regulation, may reduce the ability of environmental taxes or charges to produce the intended shifts in consumption or production. Some spending programmes may already be in place before the ecotax is introduced, and the appropriate tax rate will depend on whether such programmes are eliminated. Correction of market failures caused by government intervention, such as distorting subsidies, is important if environmental

Table 1.1. **Examples of Current Tax Provisions with Negative Environmental Effects**

Parking Space	Free (or reduced costs of) parking space provided by employers is not included as taxable income (benefit in kind).
Company Cars	The use of company cars for commuting to the place of work is not considered a taxable benefit.
Deductibility of Commuting Expenses	The costs of commuting may be deductible from taxable income and there is no distinction made between the use of public transport and private cars.
Reimbursement of Commuting Expenses	Tax-free reimbursement of commuting expenses (whether by car or by public transport) is possible in a number of OECD countries where reimbursement by the employer (based on home to work distance) to an employee travelling in his or her own car is allowed free of income taxation.

Source: OECD.

13

policies are to be properly integrated with sectoral policies. It has been estimated that if the implicit subsidy from the exemption from income taxation of the transportation benefits provided by employers to employees for commuting were removed, emissions of carbon in the United States would be reduced by 19 million of tons of carbon a year by 2010. It was estimated that requiring vehicle users of parking and of highways to pay the full cost of these services would stabilise carbon emissions in the transport sector and would obviate the need to introduce carbon taxes if stabilisation in this sector is the policy objective (Shelby *et al.*). In a more extreme case, a World Bank study published in 1992 (Larsen and Shah) estimated that the elimination of subsidies to the energy sector would have the same emission reducing effect as an OECD-wide carbon tax ranging from $50 to $90 per ton of carbon. Reduction in subsidies should be part of a policy package to reduce CO_2 emissions, but their removal is not a prerequisite for the introduction of environmental taxes. Taxes can reduce the detrimental effects of subsidies that may be politically difficult to remove. Nevertheless, government intervention is needed to achieve other policy goals, such as equity and energy security. Policies must take these other objectives into account.

1.6. Scope of the report

This report builds on earlier OECD work in this area. Chapter 2 draws on the experiences of Member countries implementing or attempting to implement environmental policies. A number of design questions – such as how to determine the appropriate tax base and tax rate – and administrative and compliance issues are addressed. The question of ''tax packaging'' is approached by first considering what can be done to reduce non-price barriers – such as lack of information and technology transfer – and then the use of tax revenues. The impact on competitiveness and trade, on the income distribution and the issue of revenue recycling are covered in subsequent chapters.

Chapter 3 provides a comprehensive overview of the mechanisms by which ecotaxes can affect trade, at both the microeconomic level – where some sectors or firms may be more adversely affected than others – and the macroeconomic level, where trade balances and trade patterns may change. The factors that may determine the impact of ecotaxes on competitiveness and trade flows are reviewed. The chapter then considers issues of ''leakage'' and policy effectiveness; that is the potential relocation of production to other countries with no, or less stringent, environmental policies. The potential for miti-

gation and compensation to alleviate the effect of environmental taxes on domestic industry and for positive impacts on competitiveness by encouraging technological innovation is explored.

Chapter 4 draws in part on earlier OECD work on the distributional effects of environmental taxes. It does not attempt a complete review of the numerous empirical studies, but assesses how compensation schemes can reduce the burden on those most affected by the tax, while preserving its cost-saving potential.

Chapter 5 explores how environmental tax revenues could be used to promote growth and employment. Some revenues will be required to alleviate the impact on trade and competitiveness and on those groups most affected by the tax, as discussed in the previous chapters. The chapter examines how the revenues from the ecotax could be used to reduce the overall tax burden on labour and other factors of production, thereby compensating for the potential loss in employment resulting from the ecotax.

The final chapter draws a number of conclusions from the preceding discussion. It summarises a number of policy options open to governments implementing environmental taxes, and reviews the trade implications, distributional impacts and employment effects.

Notes

1. There is also the danger that the use of tax provisions for environmental purposes may open the way to demands for special treatment of specific activities, and this would be contrary to the spirit of the tax reform of the last decade whereby special tax provisions were eliminated so as in increase the taxe base and reduce the tax rate.

2. Current tax systems were created to provide revenues to governments which in turn provide services to the public. All types of taxation, whether of personal or corporate income, and any types of consumption taxes, value added tax (VAT) or excise taxes, all have a potential impact on the environment, since in most cases they change relative prices between goods and inputs, between work or leisure, or between consumption and savings. In fact, given that most tax systems are the result of ever evolving tax systems that include a number of measures reflecting industrial or social policies, whereby may tax preferences are provided, existing tax systems generally create distorsions that lead to a less efficient economic system. The impact on the environment, whether beneficial or not, is in this case unintentional.

ANNEX TO CHAPTER 1

Table A.1. **Overview of environmentally-related taxes and charges in OECD countries**

As from 1/1/95

Environmental Tax Measures	Australia	Austria	Belgium	Canada	Denmark	Finland	France	Germany	Greece	Iceland	Ireland	Italy	Japan	Luxembourg	Mexico	Netherlands	New Zealand	Norway	Portugal	Spain	Sweden	Switzerland	Turkey	United Kingdom	United States
Motor Fuels																									
Leaded/Unleaded (Differential)	●		●		●	●	●	●		●	●	●		●	●	●	●	●	●	●	●	●	●	●	
Diesel (Quality differential)					●	●										●		●			●				
Carbon/Energy taxation					●	●												●			●				●
Sulphur tax																		●			●				
Other excise taxes (other than VAT)	●	●	●	●	●	●	●	●	●		●	●	●	●	●	●	●	●	●	●	●	●	●	●	●
Other Energy Products																									
Other excise taxes	●	●	●		●	●	●	●	●		●	●	●	●	●	●		●	●		●			●	●
Carbon/Energy taxation					●	●										●		●			●				
Sulphur tax					●		●											●			●				
NOx charge							●														●				
Vehicle Related Taxation																									
Sales/Excise/Regist. tax diff. (cars)			●	●	●	●	●	●	●	●	●	●	●		●	●		●	●		●	●	●		●
Road/Registration tax diff. (cars)			●	●	●					●	●	●			●	●		●		●	●	●	●		
Agricultural Inputs																									
Fertilisers																		●			●				
Pesticides					●	●												●			●				
Other goods																									
Batteries			●		●																●				
Plastic Carrier Bags			●		●																				
Disposable containers										●															
Tires	●				●	●				●								●							●
CFCs and/or halons				●	●																				●
Disposable razors			●																						
Disposable cameras	●		●																						
Lubricant Oil Charge						●																			
Oil Pollution Charge						●												●							
Direct Tax Provisions																									
Env. Investments/Accelerated depreciation	●			●	●	●	●									●		●	●	●					●
Employer-paid commuting expenses part of taxable income	●				●	●		●											●					●	●
Free parking part of taxable income	●																				●				●

Table A.1. **Overview of environmentally-related taxes and charges in OECD countries** *(cont'd)*

As from 1/1/95

Environmental Tax Measures	Australia	Austria	Belgium	Canada	Denmark	Finland	France	Germany	Greece	Iceland	Ireland	Italy	Japan	Luxembourg	Mexico	Netherlands	New Zealand	Norway	Portugal	Spain	Sweden	Switzerland	Turkey	United Kingdom	United States
Commuting expenses deductible from tax. income *only* if pub. transport used																									●
Air transport																									
Noise charges	●		●				●	●								●		●	●		●	●			
Other taxes				●														●							●
Water Charges and Taxes																									
Water charges	●				●	●	●	●		●					●	●		●	●	●	●		●	●	●
Sewage charges	●				●	●		●							●	●		●	●					●	●
Water effluent charges	●						●	●																	
Waste Disposal and Management Charges																									
Municipal waste	●	●	●	●	●	●	●	●		●	●	●				●		●	●	●	●	●	●	●	●
Waste disposal charge	●		●		●		●	●								●		●	●	●		●		●	
Hazardous waste charge	●					●	●	●		●								●	●						●

Source: OECD (1995): *Environmental Taxes in OECD Countries*, OECD, Paris, 1995, and country notes.

17

References

BARDE, J.-Ph. and K. BUTTON, *Transport Policy and the Environment: Six Case Studies*, Earthscan Publications, London, 1991.

EUROPEAN COMMISSION: ''The Climate Challenge: Economic Aspects of the Community's Strategy for limiting CO_2 Emissions'', *European Economy*, Commission of the European Communities, Directorate for Economic and Financial Affairs, No. 51, May 1992.

LARSEN, B. and A. SHAH, ''World Fossil Fuel Subsidies and Global Carbon Emissions'', Policy Research Working Paper Series 1002, October 1992, World Bank.

OECD (1989), *Economic Instruments for Environmental Protection*, OECD, Paris.

OECD (1991), *Environmental Policy: How to apply Economic Instruments*, OECD, Paris.

OECD (1992), *Climate Change: Designing a Practical Tax System*, OECD, Paris.

OECD (1993a), *Taxation and the Environment: Complementary Policies*, OECD, Paris.

OECD (1993b), *Environmental Policies and Industrial Competitiveness*, OECD, Paris.

OECD (1993c), ''Environmental Taxes in OECD Countries: a Survey'', *Environment Monograph No. 71*, OECD, Paris.

OECD (1994a), *Managing the Environment: The Role of Economic Instruments*, OECD, Paris.

OECD (1994b), *The Environmental Effects of Trade*, OECD, Paris.

OECD (1994c), *The Economics of Climate Change: Proceedings of an OECD/IEA Conference*, OECD, Paris.

OECD (1994d), ''Taxation and the Environment in European Economies in Transition'', OCDE/GD(94)42, OECD, Paris.

OECD(1995), *Environmental Taxes in OECD Countries*, OECD, Paris.

SHELBY, M., *et al.*, ''The Climate Change Implications of Eliminating U.S. Energy (and Related) Subsidies'', October 1994. Draft report prepared for the Group on Energy and Environment.

Chapter 2

DESIGNING AND IMPLEMENTING ENVIRONMENTAL TAXES

2.1. Background

This chapter reviews the issues related to the design and the implementation of environmental taxes. It focuses on the use of environmental tax instruments to reduce pollution, and not other externalities such as landscape disruptions and loss of biodiversity, as pollution is the most widespread application of ecotaxes to date. The chapter draws upon the experiences of OECD countries, particularly the Netherlands, Norway and Sweden. Each of these countries has implemented various environmental taxes, including some form of carbon tax, and have reviewed for this report the key issues and policies of their implementation strategies. Other countries, like Belgium, Denmark, Finland, Switzerland and the United Kingdom, have also introduced new environmental taxes. Certain other countries have met great opposition which either led to the postponement, modification or withdrawal of their proposal. For instance, after three years of debate, the proposal by the European Union (EU) to introduce a carbon/energy tax has recently been modified to introduce some degree of flexibility for Member countries in order to overcome the obstacles that have so far prevented its adoption.[1]

2.2. Developing an appropriate policy framework

Each environmental problem is different and presents various characteristics that will lead to the choice of one instrument, or a combination of taxes and regulations, and a different implementation strategy. These characteristics include market related features: the price elasticity or the availability of alternatives, the potential for technological innovation, the extent abatement costs might differ across sectors, the extent domestic sectors are in a favourable competitive position or in a fast growing market, or the market structure itself (competitive or oligopolistic markets). Other characteristics include environment related features such as the seriousness of environmental damage, or whether detrimental emissions arise in a certain local area or at certain time during the year or day. For instance, emissions of nitrogen oxides are more serious under certain conditions such as during hot summer days or when mixed with other pollutants like volatile organic compounds. Each

environmental tax instrument carries its own limitations and its effectiveness will depend on the circumstances and the type of pollution problem it is attempting to solve.

Environmental taxes rely principally on two types of instruments: one which is directly related to the environmental externality, say polluting emissions, and one which relies on the indirect relationship between the tax base and the externality or the pollution emitted. Tax reliefs are discussed more in the context of compensation or as complementary to the environmental tax itself. Referring to emission oriented taxes, the use of taxes on measured levels of polluting emissions is less appropriate and may not be feasible when the sources are small, varied and too numerous for individual monitoring and collection of the charge. Emission taxes are best when the pollution is local, since it would likely require locally targeted measures. Product taxes charged on inputs raises issues that are distinct from those involved in the taxation of measured emissions – including questions of integration and compatibility with existing tax policies and administrative procedures. Product charges can be particularly effective when applied to products that are consumed or used in large quantities and in diffuse patterns. Overall, when pollution is associated with consumption, taxes on products will likely be efficient, but direct taxes on emissions at the producer level will be more efficient.

The objective of environmental taxes may also differ. Taxes might be introduced to reduce consumption of the polluting good down to a level considered "sustainable". For instance, a tax on carbon might be introduced to bring carbon emissions down to 1990 levels by the year 2000, or a tax might be imposed on water emissions to ensure the survival of some fishery. Other taxes might be implemented primarily to raise revenues. Environmental taxes may also be introduced to replace and/or complement existing regulations and benefit industry if it reduces compliance costs. The tax differential between leaded and unleaded gasoline (accompanied by regulations), has resulted in several countries to the complete or near complete elimination of leaded gasoline. Their effectiveness could depend, however, on many factors, particularly the link between the tax base and the externality, and the level of acceptability of the instrument. Each of these issues is discussed below.

Linkage

A direct and clear link between the tax and the environment damage is key to the widespread acceptability of the tax and to proper market signals. The effectiveness of an environmental tax in achieving an efficient reduction in environmental damage depends on the degree to which the tax is closely linked to the environmental damage which it aims to control. The "linkage" issue is an important consideration in choosing between a system where measured emissions are taxed and a system where products are taxed. The linkage is direct in the case of an emission tax, but in the case of a product tax, the linkage is most likely indirect, and the design of the tax may become quite complicated. The case of disposable cameras in Belgium is interesting in this regard. In order to properly link the environmental damage, that is the build-up in landfill sites, to the actual detrimental disposal of the cameras, an additional measure had to be taken: if taxpayers can prove that 80 per cent of the spare parts of the cameras are actually re-used or recycled in cameras of the same type, the ecotax does not apply (De Clercq, 1994).

Where the linkage between the tax base and the environmental damage is weak, the tax may fail to induce polluters to change their behaviour, and the tax may simply become the cause of more market distortions. Appropriate information should accompany the introduction of the tax to ensure polluters understand why the tax is being introduced and what are alternative less polluting forms of consumption or production available. Issues like linkages and the effectiveness of ecotaxes in reducing pollution in fact relate to the extent policy makers use a comprehensive approach to policy making.

A comprehensive approach requires policy-makers to have a good understanding of the life-cycle of polluting products or emissions, including production techniques, substitutes in consumption, and techniques available to reduce emissions and residues. Since emissions may arise at various stages of production, a tax on just one source may not be appropriate. An input tax may give broader coverage of different sources of pollution, but will not give incentives to introduce end-of-pipe technology, if available. One possibility is a combination of policies, where the receipts from an input tax are returned to the taxpayer if end-of-pipe technologies are used. One example is the sulphur graduated duty on fuel in Norway, reflecting the potential emission of SO_2 by combustion, which is combined with reimbursement of the tax payment corresponding to the quantity of sulphur that is not emitted into the air. However, reimbursement requires a system for documentation of installed cleaning technology and supervision to ensure that cleaning procedures are implemented. This increases administrative costs. In Sweden, a tax on the sulphur content of coal, peat and petrol at a rate of 30 SKr per kilo of sulphur was introduced in 1991. Taxpayers who reduce sulphur emissions by cleaning may be reimbursed after an application to the National Tax Board [see *The Swedish Experience...*].

A comprehensive approach would also avoid situations where polluters can reduce the tax base, and so their tax payments, without reducing polluting emissions. As the relationship between the tax base and pollution must be stable, policy-makers need to understand the full production process and any alternatives, and whether emissions are similar between production techniques. In

---

Box 2.1. "PIGOUVIAN" TAXES: EMISSION OR PRODUCT TAXES?

Pigouvian taxes are well accepted in theory as economically efficient and environmentally effective instruments. In the case of pollution, a Pigouvian tax is one imposed on units of emissions, with the tax rate equal to the marginal social costs of pollution evaluated at the socially acceptable level of emissions. Pigouvian taxes may be imposed on metered emissions (for example, of sulphur) or on the detrimental effect of the use of a product. For instance, the rate of taxation on disposable cameras should be associated with the build-up of waste in landfill sites. The full tax should be applied if no part of the camera is re-used or recycled, with a lower rate if some parts of the camera are re-used or recycled.

To make a product tax truly "Pigouvian", it is necessary to collect information on the relationship between the product and the detrimental emissions, which is not always easily available. In most cases, the relationship is not very well known, so the product tax is a second or third best solution. The degree to which a tax is really Pigouvian depends essentially on whether it is possible to quantify the marginal social cost of emissions.

The number of environmental concerns that require action and the amount of information needed to set the right "Pigouvian" tax mean that this approach is likely to be too cumbersome in practice. There may be a large number of taxpayers providing negligible amounts of revenue and so the costs of collecting the tax may not be warranted. In many cases, indirect taxes on commodities or inputs may be more feasible than emissions taxes.

addition, the tax should not displace pollution problems, say from one of air pollution to one of land pollution. If it does, additional action may be necessary. There may also be beneficial environmental side effects. For instance, a tax on road fuel to reduce CO_2 will reduce other emissions such as NOx, CO, VOC and particulates.

There may be failures in other markets which prevent the effective use of environmental taxes. Taxation of chemicals or fertilisers may reduce their intensive use but might encourage extensive farming and lead to the clearing and cultivation of marginal forest lands, especially if farmers are not compensated for their contribution to a natural landscape. Other market failures, which may be created by government action or inaction, must be taken into account in designing the environmental policy package.

Acceptability

Stakeholders need to be convinced first, that there is an environmental problem requiring action and second, that the advocated policy will contribute efficiently to its solution, for a new tax to be accepted. It is important, therefore, that the link between the tax and the environmental problem it aims to solve is clear. Governments should ensure that the public in general, and those affected by the pollution and the ecotax, have feedback on the effectiveness of the policy that allows periodic evaluation. The tax should ideally be predictable and relatively stable to allow polluters to plan investment in abatement technology. Simplicity and low costs of administration, monitoring and compliance are also desirable. The use of the existing tax system and accounting measures helps avoid creating an excessive burden on industry. Norway has undertaken a systematic evaluation of the effectiveness of environmental taxes, and Sweden has so far presented preliminary results.[2]

The availability of substitutes in consumption or production may help generate acceptance of an ecotax. Substitution allows producers to reduce tax payments without necessarily needing to reduce output. In Belgium, the general philosophy of the Ecotax Law (dated 1993), is that products can only be submitted to environmental taxation if alternative, more environmentally friendly products are available. For example, in the case of disposable razors and cameras, there are more durable goods that are easily available (De Clercq, 1994). But in a comprehensive approach, policy-makers should also be aware of the environmental consequences of possible alternatives. For instance, carbon-free sources of energy entail other environmental damage: wind, solar, and hydro energy require large areas of land and can be unsightly, while nuclear power creates radioactive wastes.

The recycling of revenues to those most affected by a new tax in a way that maintains its incentives may also increase its acceptability. Switzerland proposes to use one-third of the revenues from a CO_2 tax for some environmental programmes and to redistribute two-thirds to the business sector and consumers. The question of equity which is concerned with how the burden of output reduction and of tax payments is distributed among various members of society has played an important role when countries are considering environmental taxes. Despite a lower overall cost to the society than with regulation, the distributional impacts of environmental taxes, either across consumers, firms and regions, need to be considered, even more so with environmental taxation, given that polluters not only face a reduction in production and consumption as with regulation, but they also have to pay taxes. While the tax payments can create large distributional effects, these can to some extent be offset by the way in which the tax revenues are used.

Consultation with stakeholders may ease implementation, although it is unlikely to placate all the opposition. For example, it may be difficult for a country to implement alone a carbon tax to combat global warming, particularly when the country in question contributes only a small share of global carbon emissions. By reducing consumption of fossil fuels, ecotaxes can reduce smog in cities as well as greenhouse gases, and reduce reliance on energy imports and the need to invest in new infrastructure. Highlighting these benefits will contribute to the acceptance of the tax. Consultations can take several forms, as experience in Member countries indicates: both *ex ante* commissions where parties are involved in the design of the new tax and *ex post*, where the implementation and results of the tax are evaluated.

Implementation of environmental taxes requires a detailed knowledge of the sector concerned. These data may not be known to the administration, who may have to rely on inputs from industry. This may give rise to so-called "regulatory capture", where the regulated sector has undue influence over the regulatory authorities. Many regulatory variables, such as time periods, exemptions, stock and import treatment, definition of products, could serve *de facto* as barriers to entry. Not all parts of the industry may get fair representation during the consultation process: importers and smaller firms may not be as successful at making their concerns known as larger, domestic players. Not only may representatives of domestic industry ignore the interests of foreign firms, but they may also advocate measures serving as hidden import barriers (De Clercq, 1994).

There are many actors to consider: small and medium enterprises, large enterprises and multinationals, employees, consumers, environmental groups and local policy-makers. Wide consultations are required to ensure fair representation of these different groups. Consultation may also increase awareness among polluters of how their activities interfere with the environment, potentially improving the efficiency of the tax if it prompts voluntary reductions in pollution (perhaps at no extra cost). Consultation may be perceived as a two way process, an exchange of information between the authorities and the polluters. The information generated by the consultation process also may generate public support for the policy. Companies that are perceived as more environmentally friendly than their competitors would then find new market opportunities.

The acceptability of a new tax will be affected by the institutional framework: the legal and the tax systems. The OECD Polluter-Pays-Principle and supranational treaties may limit the application of economic instruments by treaty parties and the mechanisms that can be used for enforcement. The international trade rules of the WTO may also restrict the range of tax options and other policies, such as subsidies and border tax adjustments.

2.3. Designing environmental taxes

The design of an environmental tax depends on the objectives pursued. All environmental taxes are designed to have a behavioural effect, but they are often complementary to regulations or seen primarily as revenue-raising instruments. In any case, questions of design and administration are the key to effective implementation. Design issues comprise the choice of the tax base, including the point of imposition, and the rate structure. Administrative factors relate to the assessment and collection of the tax. There may be a trade-off between the most appropriate tax base and the feasibility of the tax, as administrative costs rise as the tax base is more precisely defined. The tax rate needed to achieve a target level of abatement may be unknown because of uncertainty over polluters' short- and long-term responses, and the degree of technological innovation in pollution abatement.

The tax base and the point of imposition

The appropriate tax base and the point of imposition or of collection will depend on whether the problem is local, regional or global. Ideally, all emissions related to the pollution problem should be included in the tax base. The base will differ between pollution arising from production or consumption. The number of polluters and whether the source of pollution is diffuse or point-source will determine the optimum point of imposition of the tax.

An essential first step in choosing the tax base is a clear understanding of the life cycle of the pollutant – how it is produced, used, and disposed of – to identify activities posing significant risks. This allows a distinction between polluting activities that need action and those that are relatively safe. Environmental and health risks of polluting substances may vary according to how and where they are used. The problem may be more acute in particular localities, due to concentration of population or the geographical position of the area.

Policy-makers may also need to have a good knowledge of the cost functions of polluters in different areas. It may be more advantageous, for some reason, for all local firms to pay the tax rather than reducing pollution, so that the general tax rate may not be sufficient to reduce pollution to an acceptable level in that particular area. The tax may then need to be raised or supplemented by other environmental policies. In the case of global warming, it may not matter much if emissions in some areas are not reduced and that firms prefer to pay the tax, because climate change is not a localised problem. In this case, countries as a whole need to meet their targets. If targets are not met, it could mean that tax rates need to be increased.

The choice between an emission and a product tax will depend on the cost and feasibility of monitoring. When pollution is emitted from large, stationary sources, an emissions tax will be easier to implement than for numerous and diffuse sources. In the latter case, it will be more effective to tax associated products, if a direct link between the polluting substances and the consumption of the products can be established. For instance, carbon dioxide is emitted in strict proportion to the amount of fossil fuel burned, and there are no technologies for capturing carbon dioxide after combustion. Quantities of fossil fuels are also easy to measure, and since many are already subject to tax, the institutional infrastructure is already adequate. Other examples in this category include virgin pulp and paper and phosphates in detergents.

The choice of *point of imposition* will depend on the possibility of using the existing tax system or regulatory reporting systems. Ideally, pollution should be taxed as close as possible to the point of emission whilst minimising the number of points of collection. Thus if pollution arises from the consumption of a product, the tax should be imposed at the retail level. In the case of inputs, or if the tax is imposed early in the distribution chain (for example, at the point of extraction), then the number of transactions to be monitored is minimised. It also maximises the size of the tax base. For example, natural gas used as pipeline fuel would escape taxation if fees were collected from the end-user. In contrast, it may be preferable to impose an environmental tax at a later stage in the production and distribution chain when part of the supply of an input is imported, to avoid discriminating against a particular group of producers. In Member states of the European Union, an environmental tax should not unnecessarily obstruct the free movement of goods and services. Border controls are forbidden between European Union states, limiting application of an ecotax to imported products, which might prompt fears of a worsening competitive position among local producers.

If taxes are imposed early in the chain, there is a greater danger that the tax base will include activities that do not damage the environment. In this case, a system is needed to rebate tax payments made on these activities, but this will increase administrative costs. For example, fossil fuels also have non-fuel uses – such as making petrochemical feedstocks or certain refined oil products used in plastics production – which do not release carbon dioxide into the atmosphere and so have no effect on global warming. A tax rebate for non-polluting uses would confine the tax base to polluting activities.

Box 2.2. THE SULPHUR TAX IN NORWAY

The case of the sulphur tax in Norway illustrates the importance of using a comprehensive approach to determine the optimum policy instruments, particularly of having a clear understanding of the particularities of the pollution problem and the industry. An Interdepartmental Committee commissioned a study at the end of 1992 on the environmental effectiveness and economic efficiency of policies to reduce sulphur emissions. The study identified large differences in marginal SO_2 abatement costs for different sources, ranging from NKr 29 per kg for reduction of sulphur content of fuel oil and diesel oil, to NKr 100 per kg in the aluminum industry, following the fitting of scrubbers, and from NKr 5 to NKr 15 per kg in the ferrous alloys industry. This compares with the SO_2 tax rate of NKr 17 per kg. Three factors determine the structure of marginal abatement costs: emissions regulations, either direct limits on emissions or restrictions on certain production methods; regulations on the permitted sulphur content of fuel oil; and the range of taxes on fuel oil, including the sulphur tax.

The Norwegian study noted that the difference in marginal abatement costs might indicate a source of economic inefficiency in the allocation of abatement between polluters, although uneven abatement may be appropriate for pollution problems in given localities. In this particular case, ferrous alloys was judged to be the only industry with a significant degree of localised damage remaining. Higher marginal abatement costs in this sector, rather than the lower costs recorded, may have been appropriate. The study attributed part of the difference in marginal abatement costs between sectors to a lack of coordination between policy instruments operated by different authorities, and part to differences in the competitive position of different industries, both of which were taken into account in implementing the policy. The ferrous alloys industry had been in a weak competitive position throughout the period, and was therefore largely exempted from taking costly abatement measures required in other sectors. The study also reports that the effects of the SO_2 tax in this period were not large. (The rate of tax has since been increased.) The refunds of SO_2 tax conditional on abatement investment were therefore likely to be mainly deadweight expenditures, with little impact on investment decisions due to the low rate of the tax.

The structure of an economy and its membership of communities like the European Union need to be taken into account. Taking Belgium as an example, the 1993 Ecotax Law contains an exemption in favour of exported products which may be justified on the grounds that it is a small open economy. Furthermore, Belgium plays an important role in the distribution of goods to the rest of Europe: large quantities of goods are imported to be later exported. As a result, an exemption is granted for temporary imports. The combination of these two exemptions results in a complex set of legal provisions for imports and exports goods which made implementation of ecotaxes more difficult. Given that the European Union determines much of the structure of indirect taxes, tax provisions cannot be altered easily to accommodate the introduction of ecotaxes.

The possibility of building on the existing tax system when introducing environmental taxes is also important to consider. In Belgium, the tax authorities attempted to link ecotaxes with existing indirect taxes – including VAT, import duties and excise taxes – by stipulating that the ecotax is due the first time an indirect tax has to be paid. But a number of problems have arisen with such linkages in view of European Union rules and the free trade of goods and services within the Community (De Clercq).

How to determine the tax rate?

To internalise fully social costs, in theory, the appropriate tax rate should be set so that the marginal cost of reducing emissions equals marginal social damage. Estimating the expected value of benefits or of damages avoided involves assigning a probability to each possible outcome and a value of the environmental damage associated with that outcome. This requires a large amount of information which may not be readily available, and full internalisation of social costs requires more information than a tax designed to change behaviour or to reach a certain environmental goal. A second-best approach, then, is to set a target for environmental improvement based on anticipated responses to changes in relative prices.

Although taxes imposed directly on emissions are preferred in theory, if emission sources are not easily identifiable then a product tax may be necessary. If the relationship between the use of the product and the detrimental emissions is stable, then the outcome may be similar to a direct emissions tax. In terms of administration, the availability of data on transactions makes product taxes easier to implement. Market data can be used to estimate price elasticities, which help determine how large a tax is required to achieve a given emission-reduction target or a given revenue target. As elasticities can only be estimated, and may differ in the short- and long-run, tax rates may have to be adjusted in the light of experience, with the optimal rate reached only after some time. But unforeseen changes in rates create uncertainty for taxpayers and so should only be made when necessary.

Conflicts could arise between finance and environment departments if the objectives of the tax are not clear. For instance, a tax which is successful at reducing polluting emissions will necessarily lead to a decline in tax revenues from that source as pollution abatement measures are introduced (if the tax rate remains constant). This may not be popular with finance departments planning the expenditure programme. This problem is obviously more acute if ecotaxes represent a large share of total revenues. In most cases, ecotax revenues remain well within the regular fluctuations of tax revenues due to economic cycle. At the same time, a tax that provides a continuous flow of tax revenues may not be popular with environment officials since it could mean that the tax rate is not high enough to generate incentive effects. Short- and long-term environmental objectives of the tax should be made clear.

There may not be a conflict between environmental and revenue-raising objectives. As environmental taxes discourage the use of the polluting product, they encourage the use of environmentally friendly substitutes, if available. This may be explicit – for example, the tax differential between leaded and unleaded petrol – or implicit, if substitutes are not subject to the ecotax. Some taxes may be designed to contribute to the complete eradication of a product – for example, leaded petrol – while others aim only to reduce usage. Since ecotaxes, like other taxes, have both short- and long-term behavioural effects, fiscal and budgetary planning need not be affected by environmental taxes.

A distinction between short-term and long-term effects may be necessary when choosing the tax rate. Long-term responses will be stronger because changes in the capital stock and technology may occur. If environmental objectives are long-term, the taxes may be set at a much lower rate than if results are sought in a short period, say of one or two years. Phasing-in tax increases allows producers and consumers to adjust more easily to the new tax and plan future investment. In its assessment of the effectiveness of the CO$_2$ tax, the Swedish Ministry of the Environment and Natural Resources shows that the choice between fossil fuels and biofuels for district heating plants was influenced by the tax both in new and existing plants. In contrast, the effect of the tax on other energy sectors and in the transport sector is more difficult to identify, perhaps because investment plans are on a longer term basis (see *The Swedish Experience...*)

The tax rate on products should be based both on the price elasticity of the product concerned and on the environmental objective. Among substitutes, the taxes should be differentiated according to the polluting content of the product, in a similar way as a carbon tax would be based on the carbon content of different fossil fuels. In some cases, the product as a whole is a threat to the environment, not part of its contents: for instance, Belgium decided to tax disposable razors and cameras to encourage the use of reusable alternatives.

Since the pollution associated with the production or use of a particular commodity will be a function of the quantity of the commodity rather than its value, the tax should be specific (per unit) rather than *ad valorem*. At any particular point in time, the incentive effects of *ad valorem* and specific taxes are in theory the same. However, because product characteristics differ between manufacturers, *ad valorem* taxes may induce manufacturers to reduce prices by lowering quality instead of reducing the related emission. Under such circumstances, specific rates may be more appropriate since they do not affect quality.

The incentive effect of a specific tax may however be eroded in times of inflation. To avoid this effect, the specific rate may be re-examined periodically, and if necessary readjusted to reflect changes in the external costs of pollution. Caution should be exercised with automatic indexation procedures, particularly for economically important taxes. Policy-makers should consider the macroeconomic context and the potential effect of increasing environmental taxes. A periodic revision of rates may be sufficient, especially if long-term environmental objectives are set. Environmental taxes will also need regular reviews to assess whether they fulfil the intended purpose. Even without changes in the general price level, it may be necessary to adjust the rate because of changes in relative prices of the taxed and non-taxed substitutes (or complements).

If it is decided that the tax should be at a relatively high rate, it may be possible to introduce the ecotax while minimising initial negative effects, and allow long-term planning of investment by both producers and consumers. If implementation is pre-announced, polluters may be able to reduce tax payments immediately on introduction with forward-planning. This avoids potential financial difficulties, as high investment costs and high tax payments do not occur simultaneously. For example, with enough advanced notice, polluters may be able to modify their production processes, and producers of substitutes can ensure an adequate supply. It may also be feasible to schedule a phase-in period, like the one proposed initially by the European Commission where the carbon/energy tax would reach its full rate only after 7 years. Future increases could be made conditional on whether an intermediate environmental goal is reached. The decision to change the tax rate should take into account the implications for investment.

As with regulations, an environmental tax might lead polluters to avoid the tax in unintended ways, particularly if the rate is set very high. For example, a heavy

---

Box 2.4. **EXAMPLES OF PRODUCT TAXES IN DENMARK**

In Denmark, the retail sales of *pesticides* sold in containers less than 1 kg or 1 litre is subject to a tax. The rate is 1/6 of the wholesale value including the tax but excluding VAT. The tax on imports is 20 per cent of the producer price. Pesticides sold in larger quantities are subject to a tax of 3 per cent of the wholesale price excluding discounts and VAT.

A tax is also levied on rechargeable nickel/cadmium *batteries*. The revenues from the tax are earmarked for covering the costs of a collection arrangement for used rechargeable batteries. The rate is DKr 2 per single battery and DKr 8 per battery attached to a technical device or apparatus.

There is a tax on ordinary *lightbulbs* whereas energy saving bulbs are exempt to encourage energy efficiency.

The use of *CFCs* and *Halons,* and products containing them are subject to an excise duty of DKr 30 per kg.

Plastic and paper cups, plates, cutlery etc. are taxed at a rate of one-third of the wholesale value including the tax rate but excluding VAT. Imports face a rate of 50 per cent.

Source: OECD (1995a), *Environmental Taxes in OECD Countries*, OECD, Paris.

charge on the disposal of certain substances or materials generates an incentive for polluters to look for ways to avoid paying the charge, and not necessarily those intended by the tax, such as illegal dumping of hazardous waste. In turn, advanced notification of the tax may give rise to hoarding. This could lead to some health and safety risks: for instance, households and farmers may want to stock up pesticides and other chemicals before the tax comes into effect. Controlling these types of environmentally damaging behaviour can require costly enforcement measures. The use of a tax on floor stocks may be an effective response.

Early announcement would appear to have played an important role in reducing pollution in the case of two policies introduced by Germany (the Abwasser-ababengesetz, AbwAG, and the Wasserhaushaltsgesetz, WHG) and which are related to water pollution. Based on a study on their effectiveness in reducing environmental damage, where 92 enterprises and 46 municipalities were surveyed during the 1974-1979 announcement phase of the AbwAG, it was found that three quarters of the enterprises and two thirds of the municipalities had increased, accelerated or modified their water pollution abatement under the combined pressure of the expected introduction of the measures in the AbwAG and WHG [OECD (forthcoming)]. The NOx charge in Sweden is another example where early announcement triggered pollution abatement investment even before the tax was introduced (see Box 2.3).

It may also be helpful if governments announce targets and schedules in terms of environmental objectives, such that when targets are not met (either because the tax rate is too low or enforcement lax) the polluters know that they will have to face even larger costs in the future if they have not yet complied. Industry need to be well informed of longer-term as well as short-term targets. This provides some political commitment in the long term and certainty to firms which enables them to make provisions for these targets in their long-term investment plans. However, this may lead to a trade-off between the advantage of providing long term certainty and the advantage of being able to adapt objectives smoothly to technological progress.

2.4. Administrative and compliance issues

While regulations may entail administrative costs, the cost of applying an ecotax could be just as important, and that may require compromises between environmental effectiveness and the need to use cost-effective means of administering the taxes. The administrative costs and the effectiveness of the tax will depend in part on which level of government and which ministry is responsible for administering the tax, ensuring compliance and applying penalties, and monitoring environmental progress. The details of the administration of the tax are likely to determine not only the effectiveness of a tax, but also its acceptance. A complex administration that requires large compliance costs may lead to widespread objections to the tax. The main issues relate to the choice of the authorities responsible for administering the tax, to the monitoring requirements and to the administrative and compliance costs to both the authorities and the polluters. Each issue is discussed in turn below.

Regulatory authorities

A major issue related to tax design and implementation strategy is the need to consider the potential tax and environment policy jurisdictions: local, regional or national. The scope of the taxing authority affects the efficiency and effectiveness of any tax strategy. For instance, local authorities may be in a better position to develop the appropriate environmental policy to a localised pollution problem. However, as rivers or underground water often cross many jurisdictions, a number of local authorities or some higher level of government may be needed. In addition, it may not be effective for local authorities to tax some products that may be easily acquired from some other jurisdictions, since the costs of enforcement may be too high.

Similar problems were encountered by Belgium in enforcing its environmental taxes in a European Union operating without fiscal borders. As a small country within the European Union, there is a risk that in the absence of fiscal checks at the borders, quantities of untaxed products will leak into its economy. Such leakage is made more difficult with traditional excise because of an EU-wide monitoring system which includes the operation of bonded warehouses. Even though these administrative systems are costly, the cost is minor in comparison to the revenue raised. Taxes on cigarettes and mineral oils, for example, can easily justify their enforcement costs and their collection is made relatively easy. However, the situation with taxes imposed on disposable razors is different. The EU-wide agreed monitoring system is not available for this national tax and, taking into account the market structure and the way these goods are distributed, a well established national monitoring system could entail disproportionate costs (De Clercq).

Belgium also offers an example of the conflicts that could arise in federal states where power sharing with regions may not be conducive to integration of environmental policy and tax policy. Belgium is a federal state composed of three regions: Flanders, Wallonia and Brussels, which mainly deal with territory related matters, such as housing, land use planning and infrastructure. Environmental policy is mainly dealt with by the three regional governments, whereas the national government has only limited power in this respect, mainly with product standards, nuclear waste and international agreements (such as the EC directives in Belgian Environmental law). Because national governments have responsibility for product taxation, the integration of environmental considerations into the tax system is especially the task of

Box 2.5. CHARGES ON BATTERIES IN SWEDEN

In Sweden, following a Government Bill which stated that the use of mercury and lead must be gradually dismantled and the use of cadmium reduced substantially, batteries with the detrimental substances became subject to a new charge system. The charges amount to SKr 23 per kg for alkaline batteries and mercury oxide batteries, SKr 25 per kg for nickel-cadmium batteries and SKr 40 per lead battery (6-8% of the sales price). Producers and importers must register with the Swedish National Environmental Protection Agency (SEPA), and retailers are compelled to collect/take back used batteries. In addition, the batteries can only be sold if they are properly labelled.

The income from the *lead* batteries is divided between the firms that collect the batteries and those that recycle the lead. Administrative costs are about the same for the firms as for the government, *i.e.* 1% of the total revenues of SKr 42 million in 1992. In the same year, there was more than 360 000 batteries collected above those that were sold. The charge itself does not reduce consumer demand as there is no substitute available, but it encourages collection and recycling. Moreover, administrative costs are relatively low. As a result, a Nordic project has been set up to coordinate the collection and recycling of used lead batteries in Denmark, Finland, Norway and Sweden, which is expected to be more cost effective.

Since the charge on small batteries containing NiCd reached only about half of those sold in 1992, special initiatives were taken to improve compliance. A system of collection premiums is also being considered. Administrative costs for the SEPA have been estimated to SKr 0.3 million. The environmental problem resulting from these batteries seems to be diminishing as less harmful alternatives become available.

Source: The Swedish Experience: Taxes and Charges in Environmental Policy, Ministry of the Environment and Natural Resources, Stockholm 1994.

---

he federal government, but the regional governments have to be involved somehow since they are mostly responsible for environmental policy. Moreover, most aspects of indirect taxation are governed by the regulatory framework of the European Union (De Clercq).

When it comes to monitoring the application of the policy, the wide experience of the indirect tax departments seems to weigh in their favour particularly with regard to product taxes, either at the consumption or production level. A major advantage of this approach is that excise officers will be able to avail themselves of the same powers of entry, search and seizure which for centuries have been available to officers operating the traditional excises. Secondly, the excise taxes on petroleum products which could be considered proxies for carbon taxes in most countries are already administered by indirect tax departments. Thirdly, as some important environmental taxes will require international coordination and may involve border taxes, the indirect tax department may be best placed to conduct and administer the border taxes, if required.

Problems have however been encountered in applying the laws and procedures of traditional excises to environmental taxes. In Belgium, producers and consumers built up stocks of soon-to-be-taxed products, leading to arbitrary effective tax rates, far lower revenues than expected, disillusionment with the tax reform itself, and the development of a group of aggrieved taxpayers who had failed to exploit the loophole. These problems could be addressed with a tax on stocks – as in the proposed BTU tax in the United States – or by a gradual introduction of the tax. By and large, given their long experience of quite tight control of products, excise officials are more likely to be able to deal with the problem of pre-tax stocks than other administrations. In the United Kingdom, Customs and Excise have powers to restrict the delivery of high duty excise goods such as tobacco, alcohol and oils to homes for a period of three months prior to the Budget.

Although using the existing tax structure may indeed reduce compliance and administrative costs, there may also be important disadvantages to the use of an existing tax structure especially if there are many exemptions to the current tax, based on social or economic grounds. Before using an existing tax structure, all related tax provisions should be considered because they may lead to ineffective environmental taxation.

When the tax requires monitoring of emissions, the Environment Department may be better equipped to choose the necessary monitoring and measurement instruments to estimate emissions, and to determine where in the production process polluting emissions occur. It will be necessary for the Environment Department and the Finance Department to co-operate in order to determine the appropriate tax rate, as the rate should reflect all costs associated with the pollution, some being of an environmental nature, and others being of an economic and financial nature. Reports on environmental improvements and effectiveness may be prepared by the Environment Ministry.

Monitoring

Monitoring systems are essential not only to provide a basis for levying taxes, but also for evaluating environmental and economic impacts of the taxes. Monitoring requirements for environmental taxes may be quite similar to regulation, particularly when one compares standards based on emissions and an emission tax. Availability of the technology to measure emissions is obviously key to the success of such measure.

Adequate monitoring systems are needed to provide an accounting basis for levying pollution taxes and to evaluate the impact overall pollution levels and taxpayers. Monitoring systems must be able to calculate the amount of pollution emitted from specific sources or the amounts of toxic substances sold or used. If overall levels of the pollution remained above target levels after the implementation of the tax, then the tax rate or the tax base may need to be adjusted.

There may be a need for a system where efficiency and environmental effectiveness of the tax can be evaluated. In Sweden, a Parliamentary Commission was set up in the fall of 1993 to examine the operation of the charge on nitrogen oxide. The Commission examined the costs of the technologies used for pollution abatement, and the extent to which the abatement could be attributed to the NOx charge. Administration costs of the Environmental Protection Agency have been estimated of the order of SKr 200 per tonne of NOx abated, although part of the administrative burden can be attributed to the processes for refunding the charge revenues [OECD, (1994a)]. Norway has set in place an inter-departmental committee to evaluate the performance of environmental regulations, including tax instruments, and Belgium has established a follow-up Commission where no amendment of the Ecotax Law is possible by the Parliament without prior consultation of the Commission.

Administrative and compliance costs

For ease of administration, the number of collection points should be minimised. If imposed early in the distribution chain (at the point of extraction or importation), the number of transactions is limited and the size of the tax base is maximised. But if the product is used further down in such a way that no polluting emissions are produced (such as petro-chemical feedstocks), a system of rebates for such use will be necessary.[3] When the United States was studying the possibility of implementing the BTU tax, the tax point was initially set as early as

possible in the distribution chain. However, a variety of difficulties pushed the proposed point of imposition further and further down the distribution chain. As the BTU content may differ within energy sources, like coal, it was impossible to fix the tax rate on broad categories of energy sources. More importantly, the presence of fixed price contracts prevented the imposition of tax early in the distribution chain. In the end, the point of collection was very close to the retail level. In Belgium, taxation at the retail level is being considered in view of the fact that many taxed products are imported directly by retailers. Effective monitoring may then require labelling of each taxed product, but such a labelling scheme may entail high administrative and compliance costs.

The administrative costs of any new tax will normally be greater, the lesser the scope for the tax to be incorporated in existing systems of administration and control. The imposition of ecotaxes on currently taxed products has the advantage of not requiring any new administrative apparatus. The differentiation of the rate of existing excise taxes on leaded and unleaded gasoline found in most OECD countries is a good example. Although tax administrations may have systems of administration and control for excise duties, these apply only to a limited range of products and most firms will not be accustomed to them. Because a wider range of polluters are used to accounting for VAT, using this system may be a better approach.

Emission taxes do require the assessment or measurement of the emissions on which the tax is to be levied. The costs related to these activities will depend on the technical characteristics of the emissions (flow, concentration, stability, etc.), and the range of currently available measurement technologies. These costs will likely increase with the number of emissions sources. If some related measurement of commercial activities already takes place, there could be large savings in terms of administrative and compliance costs. These and other design issues such as penalties for non- or late-payment of taxes, the frequency of tax payments, and administrative requirements could impose relatively large costs on *small* businesses, and some adjustments may be required.

2.5. ''Tax Packaging'' issues

Given that the costs of environmental taxes are often more visible than the costs of regulations, there may be a more vocal opposition to their implementation. Environmental taxes, however, offer an opportunity to policy makers to prepare a set of accompanying policies that could make the tax not only more efficient but also more easily acceptable, in particular if they can capitalise on the increasing support for environmental goals. A comprehensive policy package should include as much as possible measures that reduce non-price barriers to effective pollution abatement, such as lack of information. In some cases, government programmes that impede the effective use of environmental taxation may have to be revised. In general, the degree of acceptance of any new tax will be partly related to what the authorities intend to use the revenues for, and if some form of compensation measures is planned. It is often in this context that the issue of environmental tax reform is raised. Some advocate that the ecotax revenues should be earmarked and used entirely to finance environmental expenditures, some being specifically targeted to a particular pollution problem or particular groups. Others argue that the revenues should be part of total public revenues, and thereby part of the general spending programme and budgetary process. In this case, some suggest that the revenues should be used to reduce government deficits, and others argue that the revenues should be used to reduce other taxes (see Chapter 5). Yet, others argue that the revenues should be used to offer some form of compensation to those mostly affected by the tax in a way that would not reduce the incentive effects of the tax (see Chapter 4). This section reviews these tax packaging issues. The degree of importance of the issues discussed in this section will depend on the relative importance of the tax base in the economy and of the ecotax revenues in government budgets, and on whether the tax aims at the reduction or complete elimination of the polluting products.

Elimination of non-price barriers

Barriers to effective pollution abatement, such as lack of information on the possible alternative inputs or consumption goods, or on the availability of pollution abatement technologies, should be eliminated. This will increase elasticities and lead to a shorter and less costly period of adjustment. A complete policy package may also include measures that promote the use of management tools such as environmental auditing, and demonstrate the potential cost savings of implementing pollution reduction technologies. The policy package may also include programmes on research and development of polluting emission abatement measures. Moreover, elimination of non-price barriers should also include a review of existing policies to avoid mixed or contradictory signals to polluters and the public. The breakdown of these barriers will make regulatory taxes more effective and more efficient.

Revenue Recycling

Given the already high level of taxation in many countries, it has been argued that any new taxes should be introduced as part of a revenue neutral package. Others argue that if total tax burden can be increased, that the use of the revenues be determined by regular budgetary and programme evaluation, and that, in this regard, the revenues may be used to reduce the deficit and public debt when this is a serious concern. Others have argued that increasing the funds allocated to expenditure programmes to ensure an effective environmental

policy is the only way that environmental taxes could be accepted. In addition, there may be a need to compensate those most affected by the tax for the tax to be accepted, and authorities might consider direct redistribution to the business community and to the general public. All these possibilities of revenue recycling present various advantages and disadvantages, which will in turn vary with the characteristics of the tax itself. In any case, the use of ecotax revenues should be determined in a context of opportunity costs, where the revenues may be used not only for environmental purposes, but also for other social and economic reasons. As the social, environmental and economic circumstances will vary over time, so may the preferred option for the use of revenues.

i) Revenue neutrality and tax reform

Revenue neutrality is often mistaken with tax neutrality where taxpayers receive exactly what they pay in terms of environmental taxes, either in the form of compensation or subsidies, or in the form of reduced tax payments related to other forms of taxation. In this section, revenue neutrality simply means that the budgetary position of governments is not changed in view of the new tax and that the overall tax burden remains the same.

It is often argued that, given the general high level of taxation in most OECD countries, that the only way that a new tax, particularly economically important taxes such as carbon taxes, will be politically feasible is if the revenues are used to reduce other taxes, that is, in a revenue neutral context. Governments face a number of options when designing a reform of the tax system, options that may or may not be used jointly. Governments may choose among a number of taxes, that is those that may affect labour costs if labour markets show some rigidities; or the direct purchasing power of households such as personal taxation or consumption taxes; or taxes that may reduce the return on capital such as corporate income taxes. Governments should first reduce the taxes that distort market signals the most and that in turn would provide the greatest improvement in efficiency and in welfare. Some countries may decide to reduce a mix of those taxes. Given that the tax systems greatly differ in OECD countries, the optimal choice will vary from one country to another (see Chapter 5). Besides, some institutional rules as in the European Union may limit the number of options available.

ii) Increasing the tax burden

The ecotax revenues also offer an opportunity to governments to increase the resources allocated to programmes – including those that deal with equity issues raised by the tax – without the amount of revenues being determined in advance for a specific purpose. The allocation of resources is then determined by the intrinsic merits and priorities of the programmes concerned. This option would be more attractive when the total tax burden is not perceived as excessive by taxpayers. Besides increasing expenditure programmes, the authorities might prefer to reduce the deficit and therefore the debt burden of future generations. A reduced public deficit and debt may increase confidence in government policy and in the economy as a whole, by creating the conditions for reduced interest rates and increased investment. Again, the preferred option will vary with the various fiscal and economic circumstances of each country.

iii) Earmarking

Tax revenues are said to be earmarked for environmental purposes if it is decided, *in advance*, that a certain share or the totality of the revenues shall be used for some environmental programmes, even if the tax is not initially set with some environmental objectives. These programmes may be complementary to the ecotax, or could be related to some other environmental problem. If tax revenues are earmarked, the amounts granted for a specific programme will consequently vary with the tax revenues and thereby will be fixed independently of regular cost/benefit analysis and programme evaluation. This may easily lead to an inefficient allocation of resources, either because the amount of tax revenues will be too large and too much will be spent on those specific programmes, or the tax revenues will be too small and not enough resources will be devoted to the programmes. In addition, depending on the price elasticities and the possibilities of new less polluting methods of production, the revenues from the ecotax may decline over time. Overall, the main argument against earmarking is that it could prevent governments from optimising the composition of government spending. In the long term, it could create inefficiencies and rigidities, and reduce the options in priority setting.

If the ecotax rate is set such that it should lead to the required level of environmental quality, earmarking the revenues for expenditures that would further reduce the targeted polluting emissions would be highly inefficient. If for some reason, it is impossible to set the tax rate to the necessary level, earmarking the revenues for programmes to help achieve more rapidly the environmental goal would make more sense. However, given that cuts in expenditure programmes are often highly unpopular, there is a danger that those programmes would survive beyond their optimal life. In any case, while resources may be necessary to help make the transition period less painful for those most affected by the tax, it does not imply that the resources have to come from the ecotax itself and not from general funding.

The risks of setting a precedent with earmarking should be carefully assessed. While there may currently be political demand to earmark the funds from environmental taxes, demands to earmark the funds from other taxes and charges could also arise for other social and development objectives, such as health and transport. As the share of earmarked funds rises, governments may find themselves no longer able to set priorities over time. This is true whether earmarking is used by local, regional or national governments. Yet, given that the fund administrators may not be fully informed of other government programmes and activities, there is a danger that earmarked funds will be allocated to activities that already receive government funding and this could lead to cross-subsidisation.

Despite these well-known caveats to earmarking tax revenues, many countries have opted for earmarking or related approaches in the case of environmental taxes, mainly in view of its political advantage. Earmarking is perceived as a instrument to increase the acceptability of the new tax, and help draw political support. Besides, the effectiveness of environmental policy may be enhanced in a context where environmental programmes are complementary to ecotaxes, and when the ecotax alone cannot achieve the environmental objectives. Many of the political advantages of earmarking (where potential political problems are seen) can be secured without the risk of inefficient allocation of resources if, instead of earmarking, governments announce at the same time as the introduction of, or increase in, an environmental tax, an increase in expenditure on environmental programmes which is financed from general tax receipts based on proper programme evaluation of the expenditure. This can establish the link in public attitudes between tax and desirable environmental expenditure, without leading to inefficient rigidities in public expenditure levels. In many cases, where revenues from environmental taxes were earmarked for environmental programmes when they were introduced, it was later decided to allocate the revenues to general budget and fund the expenditure from it with no direct fiscal relationship between the two. In other countries, this approach has been adopted from the start. In others, it has not been seen necessary to increase public spending on environmental programmes at all.

There are many cases where ecotax revenues are earmarked for some environmental purposes. In the United States, various trust funds have been set up to finance the clean-up of various contaminated sites or to finance structural expenditure programmes in the transport sectors. The nitrogen oxides charge in Sweden provides an example where earmarking could be successful in providing an additional incentive to reduce pollution, and at the same time provide some form of compensation. The NOx charge is in fact confined to a relatively small group of large sources. The measure was taken to avoid distorting the pattern of competition between the large sources and their smaller competitors. The system is operated so that almost all of the charge revenues are returned to the participating sources, in proportion to the amount of energy generated. Thus, sources with high emissions relative to their energy output are net payers to the scheme, whilst sources with low emissions relative to energy output are net recipients [see OECD (forthcoming), and Box 2.3].

The use of earmarking in the case of Economies in Transition would appear to be acceptable as a transitional measure. At present, in many Economies in Transition, environmental expenditures are largely financed by specific or general environmental funds. Such funds can be seen as effective transitional measures to catch up accumulated lags in environmental protection measures and many pollution backlogs. Environmental funds should however be seen as transitional measures. Maintaining such funds over a lasting period would eventually result in economic inefficiency. As the transition process advances, private sources and capital markets should progressively play their true role [see OECD (1995b)].

iv) The special case of user charges

Earmarking is most common in local governments when there is a direct relationship between the charge and the service provided, such as for water supply and waste removal. In fact, earmarking is a necessity in the case of user charges – as taxpayers expect a service in return. It is expected and non-controversial to allocated revenues from user charges in order to cover the cost of providing a level of service to the users. In this case the rate or fees are normally set so as to reflect the cost incurred in providing the service. Ideally, the rate of the charge and the level of resources should be determined by what is considered to be an adequate level of service, and not the inverse where the level of services is determined by the amount of revenues raised. If users need to consume more of the service, then they must pay for the additional units of service. Overall, user charges may be characterised as a direct application of the polluter(user)-pays-principle.

The risks encountered with earmarking in general, that is overspending or lack of appropriate funding, remain with user charges as well. Such programmes need to be regularly reevaluated, and should not be undertaken simply by virtue of the availability of some earmarked funds [see OECD (1995b)]. In fact, there may not be a clear boundary between taxes and user charges. If the revenues were to remain above the level of resources necessary to provide the service, then what was initially set as a user charge would effectively become a tax.

Water quality management programmes in France, Germany and the Netherlands have been set up in such a way as to generate enough revenues for various pollution-control programmes. However, their overall assessment in terms of efficiency should account for the fact that while water effluent charges are earmarked for water pollution control purposes (e.g. collective treatment facilities, sewerage, etc.), other activities comprised in those programmes in the form of investment subsidies to the private sector cannot be construed as a direct payment for services.

The charging scheme for water in the Netherlands would appear to be an example of earmarked charges leading to a level of provision of pollution abatement plants and facilities which has been dictated by the revenues generated by the charge rather than by the objective assessment of the capacity required. It has been estimated that public treatment plants in the Netherlands have surplus capacity of about 20 per cent, which might suggest that earmarking has led to over-provision. However, it is also possible that the charging scheme had greater incentive effects than expected, and that the demand dropped more than was expected. Regular and independent reevaluation of the demand for services and the charge rate could readily reduce those risks.

v) Earmarking and mitigation

In the case where it is impossible to tax emissions and a system of product taxation appears as the second-best alternative, then given that producers have no incentive to set in place end-of-pipe technologies as these would not reduce their tax payments, the authorities might consider allocating the revenues to reduce the tax bills of those producers that can demonstrate that they have effectively reduced emissions by ways that product taxes would not induce. This helps render the product tax more efficient as it provides more ways and means (even some seemingly unrelated measures, such as tree planting in the case of global warming that may act as a substitute for emission reductions) for taxpayers to reduce pollution, just like an emissions tax. This means that the payments should be limited to a small group of taxpayers, either a specific industrial sector or taxpayers in a local area, as they are more easily identifiable. This type of mitigation measure is likely to be most effective if set as a transition measure and would likely be allowed under the Polluter-Pays-Principle. However, there is no more reason to believe that the revenues have to be earmarked. They could also come from the general budget.

Distributional effects and compensation measures

Pressures for compensation or even for exemption will arise even more when the taxed product is a necessity good and represents a large share of income or expenditures, or when the ecotax increases production costs in large proportion, often where there exists few alternatives (see Chapter 4). Governments will have to consider measures to help those most affected, not only on grounds of equity and fairness, but also to ensure that opposition to the new tax is reduced. Otherwise, the new measure may be judged politically unacceptable. In any case, compensation measures may be introduced as temporary measures, and may be avoided altogether if the tax is introduced gradually. Nevertheless, compensation programmes will reduce the revenues available for tax reform, or for deficit reduction, or for undertaking additional environmental or other programmes. Again, the allocation of the revenues should be determined based on the social, environmental and economic situation in each country, and should be reevaluated regularly based on sound budgetary practices.

Caution should be exercised when designing compensation or mitigation measures to ensure that they do not affect the incentive effects of the environmental tax.

These measures may, for instance, lead to an inefficient high level of pollution abatement if the rate was already set to obtain the targeted level of environmental quality. Rebates or compensation schemes that help polluters cover pollution control costs may also reduce the effectiveness of the tax by reducing the withdrawal from the industry as a way of achieving environmental objectives. Besides, subsidies or other forms of compensation measures should not be provided for actions that would be undertaken without these measures. Overall, the need for a politically acceptable and an equitable measure will have to be balanced against the need for cost effectiveness.

2.6. Concluding remarks

There are many factors that could impede the introduction of environmental taxes. As any new tax is likely to be controversial, it would appear that the link between the tax and the environmental problem it claims to solve, should be made quite clear to the taxpayers. Taxpayers and politicians have to be convinced that the problem truly exists and that some form of government corrective measures needs to be implemented. Scientific reports and evidence would appear a necessity. Environmental objectives need to be clearly defined. Targets and schedules may be helpful in this regard as progress reports could be promised at particular points such that political commitment will not fade. As the appropriate tax rate may not be known from the start, a gradual approach may be preferable, and this will ensure lower adjustment costs. Governments may need to clarify how the ecotax revenues will be spent for the tax to be acceptable, and the optimal use of the revenues will depend on the fiscal and economic circumstances in each country. In general, strict earmarking of tax revenues, where a certain share of the totality of ecotax revenues is set aside in advance for some environmental programmes, may be associated with inappropriate levels of expenditure. Related expenditures would not be determined by the intrinsic merits and priorities of the programmes concerned, but by the availability of the revenue raised.

Notes

1. New amendments have been made to the EC proposal for a carbon/energy tax, which are intended to offer greater flexibility to Member States. However, the characteristics of the tax, the tax system and the objectives of the tax remain the same. Tax rates imposed by Member States should reach in the medium term the rates initially set in the 1992 proposal. The conditionality clause and the one on temporary suspension of the tax have now disappeared. In order to maintain the competitiveness of industry, Member States are invited to use the revenues from the tax to reduce other taxes and charges, particularly those borne by labour.

2. See *The Swedish Experience: Taxes and Charges in Environmental Policy*. For Norway, one should refer to the report published in February 1995 by the Committee appointed by the Ministry of Environment: *Instruments Used in Environmental Policy*.

3. However, it may be argued that all products carry some type of externalities, and that it should be taxed in any case. For instance, the petroleum products used to produce a plastic may release carbon emissions if those plastic bags are burnt to produce energy. In the end though, the product may bear a number of ecotaxes which when added up could lead to a tax rate way above the warranted rate.

References

BAUMOL, William J., and OATES, Wallace E., *The Theory of Environmental Policy*, Second edition, Cambridge: Cambridge University Press, 1988.

De CLERCQ, M., "The Political Economy of Green Taxes: the Belgium Experience", *Economic Instruments in Environmental Policy – in a Europe without Border Control*, TemaNord 1994:647, A Seminar Report, Denmark, 1994.

EUROPEAN COMMISSION "The Climate Challenge: Economic Aspects of the Community's Strategy for limiting CO_2 Emissions", *European Economy*, Commission of the European Communities, Directorate for Economic and Financial Affairs, No. 51, May 1992.

OATES, W.E., in OECD (1994), *Environment and Taxation: the Cases of the Netherlands, Sweden and the United States*, OECD, Paris.

OECD (1989), *Economic Instruments for Environmental Protection*, OECD, Paris.

OECD (1991), *Environmental Policy: How to apply Economic Instruments*, OECD, Paris.

OECD (1992), "The Economic Costs of Reducing CO_2 emissions", OECD *Economic Studies*, No. 19.

OECD (1992), *Climate Change: Designing a Practical Tax System*, OECD, Paris.

OECD (1993a), *Taxation and the environment: Complementary Policies*, OECD, Paris.

OECD (1993b), *Environmental Policies and Industrial Competitiveness*, OECD, Paris.

OECD (1993c), "Environmental Taxes in OECD Countries: a Survey", *Environment Monograph No. 71*, OECD, Paris.

OECD (1994a), *Managing the Environment: The Role of Economic Instruments*, OECD, Paris.

OECD (1994b), *The Environmental Effects on Trade*, OECD, Paris.

OECD (1994c), *The Economics of Climate Change: Proceedings of an OECD/IEA Conference*, OECD, Paris.

OECD (1994d), *Taxation and the Environment in European Economies in Transition*, OECD/GD(94)42, OECD, Paris.

OECD (1994e), *Project and Policy Appraisal: Integrating Economics and Environment*, OECD, Paris, 1994.

OECD (forthcoming), *Evaluating the Efficiency and Effectiveness of economic instruments*.

OECD (1995a), *Environmental Taxes in OECD Countries*, OECD, Paris.

OECD (1995b). *St-Petersburg Guidelines on Environmental Funds in the Transition to a Market Economy*, OECD, Paris, 1995.

SHELBY, M., CRISTOFARO, A., SHACKLETON B. and B. SCHILLO, *The Climate Change Implications of Eliminating U.S. Energy (and Related) Subsidies*, draft report to the OECD Group on Energy and Environment, October 1994.

SWEDISH MINISTRY OF ENVIRONMENT, *The Swedish Experience: Taxes and Charges in Environmental Policy*, Ministry of the Environment and Natural Resources, Stockholm, 1994.

Chapter 3

INTERNATIONAL IMPLICATIONS OF ENVIRONMENTAL TAXES

3.1. Introduction

The analysis of the effects of environmental policies on trade is independent of whether the emissions are transfrontier or local externalities. Trade effects should be analysed for all types of environmental taxes. In a first best world of policy choice, environmental taxes should always be introduced at the source of the externality, *i.e.* charges or taxes should be imposed directly upon the emissions or the environmental services. Yet, as seen in previous chapters, many factors can prevent the imposition of first best policies and, in practice, ecotaxes are imposed upon products or processes related to the emissions in a more or less direct way. Furthermore, environmental taxes are often accompanied by command and control measures. These environmental policy packages may have quite different impacts upon trade than direct taxes on emissions.

By imposing a positive price on the use of environmental resources, environmental taxes provide incentives for these resources to be used less and protected more. However, environmental taxes do more than this. By changing relative costs of factors of production and product prices they may affect international competitiveness of industry, and (in the case of large countries or groups of countries) the prices of traded goods and services. Furthermore, trade agreements may have implications for the effectiveness of environmental taxes, especially since they do not distinguish between taxes raised with different policy purposes.

This chapter first highlights the various key variables that one needs to consider when attempting to determine the effects of environmental taxes on trade and competitiveness. It then defines what a loss of competitiveness may mean to the firm, the industry and the country, and identifies short-term and longer-term adjustment costs. It then presents a short summary of various empirical and simulation studies on the trade effects of environmental regulations and carbon taxes. Although no empirical study has been done specifically on the subject of the broad trade effects of environmental taxes, details from several studies can be used to draw some tentative conclusions. The chapter continues with a short discussion of issues which dominate the policy debate as far as the trade effects of environmental taxes are concerned.

The widespread fear of leakage of emissions as well as of the relocation of industries into unregulated regions is discussed within the context of the available evidence. The possibilities for mitigating the impact of environmental taxes on the international competitiveness of industrial sectors and the likely environmental consequences are then assessed.

3.2. Trade and environmental taxes

The impact of environmental policy in general – and of environmental taxes in particular – on trade and competitiveness depends on a large number of factors that are described below. Predictability of the trade effects and of the effectiveness of the environmental tax becomes rather difficult when one takes all these factors into account. The key lesson here should be the need to recognise that the various circumstances surrounding the implementation of the tax and the design of the environmental tax can lead to different results, and that the specification of the situation under consideration should be made clear before policy-makers can extrapolate the results to their own situation. Without an explicit recognition of these different subgroups of possible situations, the allocative effects as well as the welfare and distributional impacts of environmental policy can not be assessed.

Some important key variables that could greatly influence trade flows and the effectiveness of the environmental policy concern whether one deals with a small country that has no influence on world market prices, or a large country where impacts on terms of trade are possible; the availability of alternatives; the point of imposition; the resource endowment of the country under study in relation to the rest of the world; the mobility of factors of production; the level of competition in the sectors; the possibilities of technological innovation; the way environmental tax revenues may be redistributed; whether trade agreements allow countries to use border tax adjustments and other trade measures to reduce the adjustment costs; and, most importantly, whether other countries implement similar policies.

Theoretical predictions about trade and allocation effects are thus not at all clear, and any models attempting to simulate trade impacts would have to be very complex. Furthermore, the data for measuring such a relationship are still scarce. The early empirical research on the impact of environmental policy on trade has generally found little evidence for a measurable relationship. One of the major problems of measuring the relationship between environmental taxes and trade is the fact that environmental taxes are generally low – in most cases probably quite below their optimal level – thus making it impossible to deduce with statistical methods the impact of optimally set environmental taxes on trade volumes and trade structure. At best, one can find the impact of current low taxes, but extrapolating these effects to higher – and presumably closer to optimal tax levels – would only be sensible if taxes and trade effects had a linear relationship. Many studies have therefore concentrated on simulation models in order to assess not yet implemented taxes at or near their optimal levels, and these models have focused primarily on carbon taxes.

Environmental taxes and competitiveness: key factors

Before reviewing key factors that would influence trade flows, it may be important to clarify what is understood by competitiveness, and some other terms such as adjustment costs in the short and long term. Countries that have an absolute cost advantage in a given range of sectors can be said to be the most competitive. Countries compete in many different ways to attract new investments. Regulations and taxation may influence long term profitability of industry and the decision to locate in one country or another. But there are many other factors influencing the decision to locate in one country: political stability, competent labour force, easy access to raw materials or to markets, and adequate infrastructure, to name just a few. In fact, while taxes in some countries may be relatively more important than in others, companies may still choose these countries because the tax revenues are used to finance infrastructure or higher levels of education that in turn reduce their costs of production. Nevertheless, some environmental taxes are bound to increase production costs relatively more for some firms or sub-sectors, at least those that use the polluting product more intensively, and firms may have to increase prices. Other taxes, such as carbon/energy taxes may affect the international competitiveness of the country in general.

As opposed to command and control regulations, ecotaxes offer more flexibility to firms to decide on the best set of alternatives to reduce production costs. However, some firms in some regions may not have easy access to alternative means of production. At the same time, while firms attempt to adjust to these increased costs of production, they also have to pay the tax, and tax revenues are usually not returned to taxpayers in a form that would totally compensate for their tax payments. If revenues are returned to taxpayers in some form or another, say by a reduction in employers' social contributions or in corporate tax, some firms (either labour or capital intensive) are more likely to benefit than others, at least in the short term.

Not all firms in one sector or sub-sector will be affected in the same way. In the case of a carbon tax, for instance, older production capacity may be less energy efficient than more recently built plants and may be more affected by CO_2 taxation. Some firms may not have easy access to less carbon emitting sources of energy. Others may be at the beginning or at the end of their investment cycle. If plans are underway to build a new plant, the new tax may simply accelerate the new investment. In fact, investment in new production capacity, at least for energy intensive sectors, may become a lot more attractive than trying to render older plants more energy-efficient. The decision to locate in other parts of the country or in another country then becomes an option. This could mean that older plants will close down and new ones will be built, using the latest, more energy efficient technologies. But new plants and new production processes may require some time to set in place and may require important sums of capital that need to be raised.

Before new capital may be set in place, some firms may encounter some cash flow difficulties, given that they have to pay the tax and that production may fall. Obviously, these problems may be more easily overcome when the economy is experiencing high growth, or when the sector itself is in a very highly competitive/innovative industry, that can easily attract new capital. Besides, when firms are experiencing a boom in demand and high profits, they may be able to offset some of the environmental tax payments if they are in a taxpaying situation. Firms that are already experiencing financial difficulties may not have taxable income that can be lowered by the tax payments, and they end up paying effectively the full ecotax (assuming that it cannot be passed forward to consumers or backward to suppliers or labour).

The impact of an environmental tax on some economic sectors may be less harmful for the competitiveness of firms if the nature of competition is on the basis of product differentiation (such as pharmaceutical products) than when firms compete on the basis of price, such as fossil fuels. The nature of the industry will also influence the decision to relocate. For instance, it may be easier to relocate or build new plants if firms are more labour intensive. The amount of capital necessary to raise may be relatively minor compared to some other industry such as in the steel industry, or oil refining. The short term and long term will obviously have different meanings for both sectors given their investment cycles.

Decisions to invest in new plants or to relocate will be more effectively taken in a climate of certainty, that is when the tax rates for the next few years are known to industry (see Chapter 2). Moreover, there may be less opposition if all firms expect to be paying the tax, than when the government lets taxpayers believe that there will be exemptions. Again, early announcement of the tax would also ease the transition period. This also depends on how the tax revenues are used and if incentives are given during the transition period. Last but not least, some industries may be less adversely affected if their main competitors are also subject to a similar tax.

The point of comparison from which effects of environmental taxes on competitiveness should be assessed can certainly affect the decision to impose a new tax. That is, should one compare the impacts of environmental taxes on competitiveness with those of some other forms of environmental policy such as regulations, or with the status quo? Generally, most models compare the impact of ecotaxes on trade with the status quo and do not consider different scenarios of revenue recycling. Moreover, most models do not take into consideration the competitive benefits an improved environment may bring to the country.

Short-term versus long-term effects

There is an important difference in the impact of environmental taxes on trade structure and trade volumes whether the short-term or the long-term adjustment by producers and consumers is included in the analysis. A short-term reaction of a firm to the imposition or an increase of an environmental tax could be a reduction in supply or a change in the input mix. For consumers, it would consist of a change in the consumption basket as well as a substitution through imports (assuming imports are not fully taxed). The long-run reaction of firms will typically involve either changes in technology, (*i.e.* innovation), or a relocation of plants, (*i.e.* capital exports), since such activities typically involve considerations with a longer time horizon.

The short term and long term effects are in fact a function of the ability of factors of production to adjust to the environmental tax by moving between sectors. This remains rather limited in the short-term such that the reduction of production in the most affected sector will not – or only to a very limited extent – immediately become compensated by an increase in production in the unaffected sectors. Consequently, the short-run will be characterised by a period where factors of production become unemployed. In the medium- and long-run, the factors of production will move from the taxed sector towards the untaxed sector. However, this move will be limited to the extent that production costs and tax payments can be reduced using innovative end-of-pipe technologies or less polluting production processes. In any case, the long run effects of environmental taxes will most likely result in larger emission reductions than in the short-run.

If innovation consists of the development of new integrated technologies, it means that domestic industry can not only reduce its tax payments, but also its private production costs. Consequently, the long-run effect of the environmental tax will not only result in a reduction of emissions as in the short-run, but it can – contrary to the short-run – improve the competitive situation of the firm

or industry under consideration. Anticipation of these longer-term effects may influence the reaction of firms to environmental policies. A structural change in an industry may provide good reason for relocation of plant, but if firms can anticipate that the costs may fall over time, the incentive to relocate will be reduced. This is even more so if firms expect that environmental taxes and standards will inevitably increase in regions where they are currently low. Governments cannot easily commit to maintaining weak standards.

In addition, because of their superior efficiency, such new technologies can become diffused to other countries even without environmental regulations in the rest of the world.[1] Indeed, the raising of standards or environmental taxes by one country may even create certain incentives for others to follow. Once innovation has taken place, the resulting products can be made available to new markets at a lower price, for the costs of R&D will have been sunk. Further, the raising of standards and environmental taxes will bring about changes not just in end-of-pipe technology but more fundamental re-designs of production processes and even of products. Hence, the technologies developed in part to meet tougher requirements in the taxing country may still be employed in other countries. The environmental tax therefore would produce positive spillovers for foreign countries in terms of an improved environment even without transfrontier pollution. Of course, this positive welfare effect in the domestic country will be amplified if transfrontier pollution problems are involved.

3.3. Trade: key factors and assumptions

Small versus large country

The basic difference between the small and the large country case is that in the former the imposition of an environmental tax may not influence relative world market prices, whereas in the latter case it could. For example, a carbon tax unilaterally imposed by a small country will not change the world market prices for steel, but the same tax imposed by all OECD countries might do so. The implications of this distinction are important. If the environmental tax is imposed on emissions from production of a tradable good in a small country, consumer prices, that are determined by the perfectly elastic world market supply, may not change so that the only adaptation in the economy will take place within the sectoral production structure. In contrast, policies implemented in a large country alone will influence supply and demand of tradable commodities on the world market such that international prices will also change. Consequently, the environmental tax will not only influence the allocation in the rest of the world, but the repercussions in the world market will again change the internal allocation in the taxing country.

Production versus consumption taxes

Another key variable concerns the question of whether the environmental effect occurs during the production or the consumption of a particular commodity and where on the production and distribution stream the environmental tax is levied. Internal efficiency would require to locate the economic instrument, *i.e.* the tax, as close to the source as possible [OECD (1991)]. Hence, polluting emissions that arise during the production process or during consumption should be taxed directly at the emitting source. In many cases a direct tax on emissions is impossible or too costly due to monitoring, control, or other problems. In these cases, taxes can be imposed upon the product either at the domestic producer level, as an input, or at the retail level. This makes an important difference since the environmental tax on externalities in the production process would be levied only on domestic production, whereas an environmental tax for correcting consumption externalities would need to be levied on domestic consumption, *i.e.* domestic production minus exports plus imports. Consequently, the trade impacts of these two different taxes can vary considerably.

A tax on consumption will by definition be a tax on domestic products only if they are sold domestically and on imports, but not on exports, *i.e.* the domestic consumer price will rise and, in the case of a small country, domestic producer prices remain equal to world market prices. The domestic demand for the taxed product will fall and that for substitutes will rise. Domestic production remains unchanged as exports increase and offset the reduction in domestic consumption.[2] Hence, a second-best policy of emission control through a tax on the consumption of the "dirty" good has only a chance of becoming effective, if the externality is indeed a consumption and not a production externality because production will not change.

National versus transborder externalities

Another dichotomy comes from the nature of the environmental effect to be investigated. If the use of the environmental resource affects the well-being of the individuals of the domestic country only, then there are no spillovers of pollution or resource use. On the other hand, if such transborder effects are present, then the optimal policy choice will be different, and will depend on whether the country follows a policy of maximising national welfare or whether it maximises global welfare.

Distinguishing between transboundary and national pollution problems is important from a welfare standpoint and in terms of spillover effects of the reallocation of production among countries. Policies towards pollution which does not cross frontiers will only indirectly change the environmental quality in the foreign country through changes in trade flows, whereas transfrontier pollution has direct spillovers as well as indirect ones. As long as only the allocation effects of environmental tax are considered, a distinction between local and transfrontier pollution is not necessary, but the effectiveness of the policy will be affected by the existence of transborder externalities. Choosing optimal tax rates or analysing overall welfare effects would require to distinguish between the two cases.

Relative endowment of factors of production

The relative factor endowments of countries determine their comparative advantage and the trade structure. A country is said to have a comparative advantage in the production of those commodities that use its abundant factors of production intensively. Environmental policies that directly limit the use of the environment or that directly raise the costs of using environmental resources will consequently change the comparative advantage of that country. Hence, by reducing the use of the environmental resource, a relatively capital or labour rich country will even increase its comparative advantage in the production of goods which use capital or labour intensively. In contrast, a country which is relatively well endowed with the resource "environment" will by imposing environmental policies reduce its comparative advantage and – in an extreme case – even reverse the comparative advantage.

Factor mobility

Factors of production can be quite mobile. In fact, only the natural environment itself can be considered an immobile factor. When factor mobility is included, the impacts of environmental taxes may be quite different, other things being equal. When there are mobile factors, environmental taxes can induce factor flows which in turn change the comparative advantage of the countries and as a consequence the sectoral production and trade structure. Environmental taxes that reduce the availability of the immobile factor environment by raising its price, may lead to an outflow of the mobile factors since the larger immobile resource endowments in the rest of the world will secure a higher marginal product of the mobile factors than in the country from which the factors have emigrated. Mobile factors of production may greatly increase the adjustment costs since the tax not only puts a price on environmental externalities, but it also reduces the supply of other factors of production. This raises the question as to whether capital is mobile within a time period comparable to that in which goods are traded. For some industries, physical capital such as equipment can be quite mobile. For other industries, capital being both location and industry specific, is rather immobile both across industries and across countries. The short and long term impact of environmental taxes on trade flows will be quite different across industries.

Factor mobility has the tendency to increase the probability that environmental taxes lead to a relocation of production facilities into less regulated regions. If the related environmental damage is local, the authorities

Box 3.1. EFFECTIVENESS OF ECOTAXES WITH BTA

The case of CFCs, identified as greenhouse gases, may help illustrate how various factors may affect the effectiveness and efficiency of an environmental tax, and how the tax may affect domestic consumption and production patterns and trade flows. In this example, it is assumed that the country introducing the tax represents a small share of world markets and thus has no influence on world prices; that the country is the only country to introduce such policy; and that the revenues raised from the tax are used in a non-distortionary fashion.

Domestic taxation of CFCs would most likely increase the production costs of refrigerators, especially if no other alternatives are easily available. That would reduce the demand for domestically-produced refrigerators, but given trade, domestic consumers will likely switch to cheaper imports. This phenomenon is known as *leakage*. If the release of CFCs into the air occurs not at the production levels but when used refrigerators are being disposed of, then domestic emissions of harmful CFC emissions will not fall, making the tax environmentally ineffective in addition to reducing domestic output. If the harmful emissions of CFCs occurred during production, then the taxing country would be successful at reducing domestic emissions of CFCs, but global emissions of CFCs would likely remain the same (and could even increase if foreign producers are not as successful as domestic producers at limiting CFCs emissions during production process). In a similar situation where environmental damage arises at the local level only and from consumption patterns, a tax imposed on domestic producers would be rendered ineffective in view of trade flows.

Countries might consider using *border tax adjustments* (BTAs), whereby taxes paid by domestic producers are reimbursed if the products are exported, and whereby taxes are imposed on imports. This assumes that BTAs would be allowed under international trade agreements and that they could easily be assessed even when pollution arises from production methods. Border tax adjustments would increase the effectiveness of an environmental tax aimed at reducing emissions that arise out of consumption patterns, but not emissions that arise out of domestic production processes. There are a number of possible scenarios, say for a small country where there are no terms of trade effects to consider:

- If the externality is local and arises out of consumption, then the tax imposed on domestic consumption (with BTAs) would be effective.
- If the externality is local or global but arises out of production processes, then the tax imposed on domestic consumption (with BTAs) would not reduce domestic emissions, since producers can sell their products offshore.
- If the externality is global and arises out of consumption, then the success of the tax imposed on domestic consumption with BTAs is limited to the extent that domestic consumption is reduced, but this is unlikely to solve any global pollution problem.

---

may welcome such a move, even if in some instances it might also mean a loss of jobs. If the pollution is more of a global nature, as in the case of global warming, such a move not only means that jobs might be lost, but that the policy does not solve the pollution problem, and might even worsen the problem if the new production facilities in the host country applies production processes that are even more polluting than those previously applied in the taxing country.

This complementary relationship between the availability of the environment and mobile factors of production introduces a strategic element into environmental policy by allowing a country to attract mobile factors of production by imposing lower environmental standards and taxes than the rest of the world. However, it is not clear how long countries may be able to exploit this

relationship in the long run. As there is a positive relationship between environmental quality and the productivity of other factors of production, the gain may be lower than expected.

Non-competitive behaviour

The impact of environmental policies on trade and their environmental effectiveness will also depend on the market structure of the economy. The results will differ according to whether one deals with a domestic monopoly or an oligopolistic market structure. In fact, given the market structure of the country, a unilaterally set environmental target by one country would most likely result in a target which is below or above that which would be imposed for environmental reasons alone.

Under imperfect competition, the strategic behaviour of firms in making locational choices as well as the impact of environmental taxes on the degree of competition within the industry can produce rising as well as falling prices in the industries facing environmental regulations. As the trade impact depends on these price changes, anything can happen after the imposition of an environmental tax and predictions can only be made by considering the exact situation of the industry, the behaviour of the firms, their technological characteristics, the degree of competition, and many more factors.

Redistribution of revenues

The redistribution of the ecotax revenues will also influence the effects of the tax on trade movements. For example, if the revenues are used to reduce the tax burden on capital or on labour, the cost of production of commodities that use those factors intensively will decrease (assuming factor prices are not rigid), and the country will either export more or import less of those commodities that use the factors intensively in view of a greater comparative advantage, while commodities that use the taxed product intensively will face a lower demand at least domestically, due to higher prices (see Chapter 5).

Overall, a permutation of all these variables produces a considerable number of combinations. It is clear that one can not predict the trade impact of an environ-mental tax without explicitly stating the particular situation of the economy and the point where the environmental tax is imposed.

3.4. Empirical evidence

Effects on competitiveness and trade

Concerns about competitiveness are important for two reasons. First, a country may wish to ensure that its *own* environmental policies do not damage its international competitiveness. Second, a country may wish to ensure that the environmental policies of *other countries* do not damage its competitiveness. Either concern may motivate the use of some mitigation measures or of border tax adjustments. These policy responses will be considered in Section 3.5. The purpose of this section is to review the evidence for effects on competitiveness.

To begin, it should be emphasised that all environmental policies have potential implications for competitiveness and trade. A carbon tax would increase costs to industry, but so would a tradeable quota scheme which limited the total quantity of carbon dioxide that can be emitted or regulations prescribing energy efficiency standards. *A priori* it cannot be ascertained which policy would have the greatest impact on competitiveness and trade. However, an important difference between

---

Box 3.2. THE CASE FOR INTERNATIONAL AGREEMENTS

Correcting for cross-border externalities requires multilateral cooperation. To take an example, protection of the stratospheric ozone layer is a global public good, such that when protected for one country, the ozone layer is protected for all. Efficiency is likely to demand that all countries reduce their emission of ozone depleting substances. However, while each country would bear the full cost of such an emission reduction programme, each would only share a fraction of the total benefit. For this reason, there may exist incentives for countries to free-ride on the abatement by cooperating countries. Free-riding not only harms the cooperating countries but also blocks achievement of an efficient environmental policy. To deter free-riding, cooperating countries may consider imposing a non-neutral border adjustment on trade in certain goods with free-riding countries. This difference is important, not least because under the rules of the international trading system GATT, border tax adjustments would be allowed for taxes imposed on consumer products but not on production processes. The objective of the tax, that is whether environmental or revenue raising, is not considered to determine whether BTAs should be allowed. Besides, it may not be possible to estimate how much imports should be taxed.

The Montreal Protocol bans trade between parties and non-parties in controlled substances (such as CFCs); bans imports from non-parties of products containing controlled substances (such as refrigerators); and contains provisions for parties to determine the feasibility of banning or restricting imports from non-parties of products produced with, but not containing, controlled substances (such as electronic components which use CFCs as a cleaning solvent). These restrictions are not analogous to border tax adjustments. They do more than correct for competitive disadvantage and leakage. They are intended to provide an incentive to countries to participate in the Protocol with a view to ensuring the effectiveness of the agreement.

nvironmental taxes and other policy tools is that, in the ase of the former, firms pay not only for the cost of protecting the environment but also the environmental ax. Therefore, while economic instruments might chieve the environmental objective at lowest overall ost, environmental taxes could still have greater impli-ations for competitiveness than alternative policies, par-icularly at the industry or firm level.

The effect of an environmental tax on competitive-ıess will also depend on how the tax revenues are mployed. Jorgenson and Wilcoxen (1994) estimate that eal GNP in the United States would rise if revenues from ı carbon tax were used to reduce marginal tax rates on apital income. Similarly, the European Commission 1994) estimates that, if carbon tax revenues were used to educe employers' social security contributions, both 3DP and employment could be higher in the long run han would otherwise be the case (see Chapter 5). How-ver, these and other studies (see, for example, Charles River Associates and DRI/McGraw-Hill, 1994) show that 3DP may also decline with the introduction of the car-on tax, depending on how the tax revenues are mployed, how large the tax is, and other factors. Of ourse, in many cases, the impact on GDP or GNP is not ı good measure of the impact on sectoral or firm ompetitiveness.

A number of research papers have attempted to letermine the effect of environmental regulations gener-ılly on competitiveness. These studies do not isolate the elationship between environmental taxes and competi-iveness specifically, but their findings are relevant to this liscussion for the reasons outlined above. Rather than eview this literature in detail, it would seem more useful o consider the conclusions reached in recent extensive urveys of this literature. This is especially so because hese surveys reach essentially the same conclusions. Dean (1992) concludes: "More stringent regulations in ıne country are thought to result in loss of competitive-ıess, and perhaps industrial flight and the development of)ollution havens. The many empirical studies which have ıttempted to test these hypotheses have shown no evi-lence to support them." Similarly, Pearce (1992) con-:ludes: "Overall, ... there is no evidence that industrial :ompetitiveness has been affected by environmental reg-ılation... [and] there is little evidence to support the 'pollution haven'hypothesis".

In general, while research on the competitiveness ffects of environmental policies is still ongoing, a sys-ematic relationship between existing environmental poli-ies and competitiveness impacts has not yet been identi-ied. While some case studies reviewed by Dean and Pearce find that the location decisions of firms are not ignificantly influenced by environmental regulations, Grossman and Krueger (1992) cite a survey by the US General Accounting Office, "suggesting that a few American furniture manufacturers may have moved their •perations to Mexico in response to the State of California's tightening of air pollution control standards

for paint coatings and solvents''. Yet, even this evidence hardly conveys the impression that environmental stan-dards systematically influence industrial location.

Similarly, while Grossman and Krueger (1992) find that the sectoral pattern of trade between the United States and Mexico has not been influenced by pollution abatement costs in US industry, other econometric stud-ies have found significant effects. Low and Yeats (1992) find that environmentally "dirty" industries have migrated over the last two decades towards lower income countries where environmental standards are weaker. However, Low and Yeats (1992) are careful to add that such migration may not have been caused by differences in environmental standards: "...data from the United States on pollution abatement and control expenditures presented in other studies tend to suggest that the evi-dence of dirty industry dispersion examined in this paper is unlikely to be adequately explained by environmental policy."

Lucas, Wheeler and Hettige (1992) find that stricter regulation of pollution-intensive production in the OECD countries may well have "led to significant locational displacement, with consequent acceleration of industrial pollution intensity in developing countries", but add: "Of course, one cannot be certain of a causal connection between [the observed growth in toxic-intensity of devel-oping countries] and the roughly concurrent shifts in OECD environmental policies. Yet the results are none-theless suggestive of a potential contributory effect."

One cannot therefore rule out the possibility that differences in environmental standards or taxes affect competitiveness – at least not in specific instances. How-ever, the literature hardly supports the view that differ-ences in environmental standards are a major source of competitive advantage. Our brief survey here thus reaches essentially the same conclusion as the most recent extensive survey on the subject (Jaffe et al., 1993): "Overall, there is relatively little empirical evidence to support the view that environmental regulations have had a measurably adverse effect on competitiveness, however that elusive term is defined. Although the long-run social costs of environmental regulation, including effects on productivity, may be significant, studies attempting to measure the effect of environmental regulation on net exports, overall trade flows, and plant-location decisions have produced estimates that are small, statistically insig-nificant, or not robust to tests of model specification."

Of course, this finding may simply reflect the fact that environmental regulations have historically affected costs very little. More ambitious policies have been pro-posed, and it is possible that these would have more significant effects on competitiveness.

To examine the effects of such ambitious policies requires simulation analysis, and a number of studies have examined the implications for competitiveness of carbon taxes. Estimates of the costs of carbon tax policies have been extensively surveyed by Working Group III of the Intergovernmental Panel on Climate Change (see Hourcade *et al.*, 1994). This survey concludes that estimates vary wildly depending on model parameters (such as energy demand elasticities and assumptions regarding the substitutability of traded goods) and the policy scenario examined (extent of reduction in emissions and extent of international co-operation). Probably all that can be said with confidence is that the effects of a carbon tax policy on competitiveness could be substantial. Since the question of competitiveness is related to the question of leakage in the case of carbon taxes, it is appropriate that a more detailed discussion include an analysis of leakage.

Environmental effectiveness and leakage issues

Governments are concerned not only about the effects of an environmental tax on competitiveness but also about the effectiveness of the policy in achieving its environmental aim. In the case of cross-border externalities, this concern about effectiveness is really a concern about leakage. Leakage, which is transmitted through trade, arises if other countries cause incremental damage to the environment as a consequence of a change in any one country's environmental policy. It should be emphasised that this response by foreign governments does not result from any deliberate policy to increase emissions. Rather, leakage results from the absence of a policy to hold emissions fixed.

Leakage refers in the context of carbon taxes to changes in carbon emissions in non-participating regions induced by abatement efforts in participating regions. If a country or region introduces a tax which changes the comparative advantage in the taxing country or region, there will likely be increased production of the taxed products that use carbon fuels inputs in the rest of world. This could lead to a substitution of imports for domestic production for imports and consequently increase emissions in the rest of the world. In the case of global pollution such as CO_2, the environmental effect of the tax in the taxing country could more or less be offset through this substitution effect. In any case, the issue of leakage should also be seen in light of the revenue scenario and of the implementation period and the level of tax rate under study.

The scope for leakages is reduced the greater the number of countries participating in an agreement. If participation is global, carbon leakage is not an issue. Based on OECD (1995*a*), there are three major effects determining the size and sign of carbon leakages, involving mechanisms that may work in opposite directions:

i) Changes in the trade structure; imposing an energy tax changes the comparative advantage in the production of energy intensive goods, entailing changes in the location of their production.

ii) Changes in world energy prices; imposing a tax on energy will reduce energy demand and thus weaken world prices which may stimulate energy demand in non-participating regions. It could also modify the structure of prices among different energy sources, inducing inter-fuel substitution in non-participating countries and thus a change in their emissions.

iii) Regional terms of trade gains and losses. Relative price changes can alter the terms of trade in each region, causing a change in emissions *via* induced real income changes. For energy exporting countries, depressed energy price reduce real incomes and thus consumption and carbon emissions compared with baseline ("negative" "carbon leakage") [OECD (1995*a*)].

The magnitude of leakage is normally reported as a "leakage rate", which may be defined as the increase in emissions by other countries divided by the reduction in emissions by the country or countries undertaking the unilateral policy. Typically, we would expect this rate to be between 0 and 100 per cent. However, it is possible that the rate could fall outside this range. For example Charles River Associates and DRI/McGraw-Hill (1994) estimate that a unilateral carbon tax ($100 per ton of carbon) by the United States would reduce foreign GDP by 0.3 per cent, relative to a baseline scenario in which the US did not impose a carbon tax. Although the unilateral policy confers a price advantage on foreign producers, the reduction in domestic demand is so great that output abroad actually falls as a result of the policy. This suggests that foreign emissions might also fall. As well Oliveira-Martins, Burniaux and Martin (1992) estimate negative leakage rates for some regions in some years.

The leakage rate might even exceed 100 per cent Horton, Rollo and Ulph (1992) consider the effects of a unilateral policy for an industry which exhibits increasing returns (fertiliser), and find that leakage is likely to be very substantial due to relocation. In fact, they argue that leakage may exceed 100 per cent, as all the firms in co operating countries move to non-co-operating countries where it is optimal to use more carbon-intensive fuel than would be the case in co-operating countries, even before the policy was implemented[3].

Despite these possibilities, studies which explicitly seek to estimate leakage typically obtain estimates which range between 0 and 100 per cent. Yet, even within these bounds estimates of leakage vary widely. It is difficult to determine the reasons for such differences, because the rates are calculated for different simulations using different models incorporating different assumptions. Rather than survey the literature, it would probably prove more instructive to compare two reports which lead to very different conclusions.

Pezzey (1992), using Whalley and Wigle's computable general equilibrium model of trade, estimates that a 20% reduction in carbon emissions within the European Union (EU) alone (relative to a baseline trend in emissions) would be associated with a leakage rate of 80%. (This is not a dynamic model, such that no time frame is specified.) In other words, for every 10 tons of carbon abated by the EU, global emissions would fall by only 2 tons. Pezzey also calculates that a 20% reduction in OECD emissions would be associated with a leakage rate of 70%. These leakage rates suggest that unilateral policy would be largely ineffective. Of course, it also suggests that competitive impacts will be great.

Oliveira-Martins, Burniaux and Martin (1992), using the OECD's GREEN model, estimate much lower leakage rates for policies aimed at stabilising carbon emissions at their 1990 levels. They estimate leakage rates for a unilateral EU policy of 11.9% in 1995 and 2.2% in 2050, and for a unilateral OECD policy of 3.5% in 1995 and 1.4% in 2050. These leakage rates suggest that leakage does not render unilateral policy ineffective.

As already noted, other studies estimate leakage rates somewhere between these two sets of estimates. However, at present, there is no consensus among economists about the magnitude of leakage. What can now be said is that leakage, like shifts in competitiveness, is a potentially serious problem for unilateral policies and for the effectiveness of the policy. Leakage is likely to remain highly debated and will remain an important disputed factor in international negotiations. The potential impact of say a carbon tax on leakage and competitiveness will differ with the magnitude of the tax involved, but also with the number of countries implementing the tax. In any case, decision makers should not lose from sight the relative magnitude of the leakage and potential emissions of carbon from the countries non-party to the agreement, and most importantly the other environmental spillover effects of increasing the price of energy and transport.

3.5. Mitigation measures

Ecotaxes can result in different cost and distributional impacts for various firms, sectors and regions, and offsetting measures may be necessary to ensure a greater acceptance of the tax. Environmental tax revenues may be used to compensate those least able to pay new taxes. A number of possible adjustments have been proposed, such as exemptions, rebates and compensation measures for the production sectors. Other measures have been advocated for the business sector where accelerated depreciation rates or refundable investment tax credits may be offered for investment in pollution abatement technology. In any case, the compensation measures should be designed as much as possible in a way that does not eliminate or reduce the economic incentives of the tax, or reduce its economic efficiency and environmental effectiveness.

Sectoral differentiation of environmental taxes

In the case of carbon emissions, for instance, an efficient tax would tax all carbon emissions the same. No distinction should be made between economic sectors, or consumption groups since each unit of carbon emissions produces the same level of damage. Nevertheless, many countries have found it necessary to provide some form of compensation or exemption. The European Commission's proposal for a carbon/energy tax exempted energy-intensive industries with a large involvement in international trade from paying the tax precisely for this reason. To the exception of Finland, countries that have actually imposed a carbon tax also typically impose smaller burdens on industry, in order to shield industry from harmful competitive impacts. Denmark's carbon tax is half as large for businesses registered under VAT law, and energy-intensive industry may be given refunds of up to 90 per cent if conservation projects are undertaken. Norway's tax was first imposed on the domestic use of gasoline and mineral oils and the combustion of natural gas offshore. The tax was later extended to include coal. Precisely because of concerns about competitiveness, Sweden redesigned its carbon and energy taxes in 1993 by exempting industry from paying the energy tax and by requiring that manufacturing industry and commercial horticulture pay only one quarter the carbon tax levied on other users.

Compensation schemes could clearly reduce the environmental effectiveness of the ecotaxes. Programmes designed to assist polluters in abating pollution may weaken the incentive effects of environmental taxes. Moreover they may lead to an inefficiently high level of pollution abatement if the rate was already set to obtain the targeted level of environmental quality. In addition, if households and producers face different prices on some fossil fuels, this may lead to considerable incentives for tax evasion by consumers posing as producers and to considerable costs of tax evasion and of control intended to curb such tax evasion. Rebates or compensation schemes that help polluters cover pollution control costs may reduce the effectiveness of the tax by reducing the possibility of withdrawal from the industry as a way of achieving environmental objectives. Moreover, compensation scheme reduce long-term social acceptance of the charge policy. If compensation schemes are felt necessary, they should avoid prescribing the type of pollution abatement technology to be used. Instead, they should let polluters choose the most cost efficient technology. Besides, prescribing a given technology could greatly add to the administrative costs of the tax.

A crude approach to reducing both the loss in competitiveness and leakage is to exempt export-oriented industries, which would be most affected by an environmental tax, from having to pay the tax. More generally, policy might differentiate the tax by sector to reflect concerns about the associated trade effects. An exemption is only an extreme form of sectoral differentiation. Exemptions that are often designed to allow heavy polluters to remain competitive, within an industry or in the international arena, not only reduce the tax burden of the said industry, but they also make less energy-intensive industry comparatively disadvantaged. Moreover, exemptions may mean that other groups end up facing a higher tax rate than the one that would be optimal in terms of efficiency if the environmental objective remains the same. It forces them to over-invest in pollution abatement and lowers the economic efficiency of the tax.

Providing an exemption from a carbon/energy tax for energy intensive industries would appear to go against the very purpose of such a tax. Oliveira-Martins, Burniaux and Martin (1992) estimate that an exemption for energy-intensive industry in the EU would have virtually no effect on either leakage rates or output of energy-intensive sectors. The reason is that, to meet the same emission target, a larger tax must be placed on the non-exempt sectors. Since the exemption forces wide differences in marginal abatement costs across sectors, the overall cost to the economy of meeting the environmental objective is increased, and aggregate output is reduced compared to the case where exemptions are not granted. Output by the energy-intensive industries is unchanged, as the gain in exports brought about by the exemption is offset by a loss in domestic trade with the non-exempt sectors. Leakage is unaffected because the non-exempt sectors also engage in trade, and the higher tax on these sectors has the effect of shifting production by these sectors abroad.

Border tax adjustments

Border tax adjustments (BTAs) involve the application to imports of domestic taxes and the remission of domestic taxes on exports of like products, and are used to neutralise the competitive effects of a domestic tax. Border tax adjustments raise three main questions with respect to environmental policy. The first one involves the extent to which BTAs can further the environmental objectives of the environmental tax. The second question involves the legal question as to whether they would be allowed under international trade rules. The third main issue involves the practicability of imposing BTAs to compensate for taxes imposed on consumption and production patterns.

With regard to environmental effectiveness, border tax adjustments on products when pollution arises from consumption patterns can actually help make the environmental tax more efficient. However, policy makers should be aware that border tax adjustments may reduce the effectiveness of environmental taxes, particularly in the case where pollution arises from production processes and methods (see Box 3.1). For instance, if the tax were to be somewhat imposed on imports and remitted on exports, domestic consumption will fall, but producers in a small open economy can still sell their products at the world price, such that exports may increase and domestic pollution does not necessarily fall. If no BTAs are allowed on imports and exports, then domestic production falls unless domestic producers can easily set in place less polluting technology to reduce tax payments and production costs. If BTAs are imposed on imports but not on exports, then at least domestic producers remain competitive within their own country, but not in international markets, and the ecotax would have some effect on domestic emissions.

On the question of whether border tax adjustments would be allowed under WT0 rules when an ecotax is imposed, the OECD Report on Trade and Environment to the OECD Council at Ministerial level (OECD, 1995b) concludes the following:

"The multilateral trade rules contain provisions relevant to border tax adjustments, *i.e.* the application to imports of domestic taxes on like products, and the remission of domestic taxes on exports of like products. WTO rules have been interpreted as generally allowing, subject to agreed disciplines, for border tax adjustments on products on the basis of product characteristics or physically incorporated inputs, but not for taxes on imports on the basis of domestic process taxes. These rules do not of course directly limit a country from using taxes to address environmental problems occurring in its own jurisdiction. However, some have expressed the view that border tax adjustments for domestic process taxes may, due to perceived competitiveness effects of these taxes, be a necessary component of countries' efforts to use these economic instruments domestically to prevent serious global environmental harm. In general, the practical feasibility, environmental benefits and potential risk for disguised protectionism associated with adjusting taxes on the basis of process or process inputs at the border are not clear and require further exploration. These issues are being addressed in the WTO in the context of its work on the relationship between trade rules and environmental taxes and charges."

There is also a number of practical problems with allowing such border tax adjustments for taxes imposed on emissions arising from production processes and methods. One is that it is technically difficult to ascertain how a product has been produced or what share of production taxes it bears. Although a GATT panel (on the US Superfund) agreed that a tax could be based on the "predominant production method", this was not a general ruling; it related specifically to the production of chemicals manufactured using feedstocks. The problem would be even more difficult in the case of a border tax adjustment for a carbon tax. Virtually all production results in the emission of carbon dioxide, and not all production is characterised by a "predominant production method". Although border tax adjustments based on PPMs would be difficult to administer in many cases, and even when they appear inconsistent with WTO trade rules, the consequences of failing to allow such adjustments must also be recognised. Where tax adjustments on PPMs are not allowed, some have expressed concern that countries may be inclined to shift environmental taxes onto products, even where environmental objectives can be achieved more efficiently through taxes on emissions.

Another problem with border tax adjustments and global emissions is that BTAs may be intended to influence indirectly the behaviour of other countries to the advantage of the country imposing the ecotax. However, the environmental tax is often designed taking only the perspective of the domestic country. This raises the question as to whether the policy is efficient, even in the second best sense. Another is whether it is fair. On the question of efficiency, it would seem that aggregate emissions could be reduced at lower overall cost if the foreign country or countries could be convinced through negotiations to adopt policies to reduce their emissions. Influencing foreign emissions, by influencing foreign output through the price mechanism would seem to be a very blunt instrument for achieving the aim of even the domestic country of reducing foreign emissions. On the question of fairness, it would seem that one should consider whether or not the foreign country or countries are free-riding on the abatement of the domestic country. If they are not free-riding, then the case for BTAs on fairness grounds would seem vulnerable.

Both of these observations point to the desirability of basing policy in the case of an international externality on a co-operative, multilateral framework. In this regard, the Montreal Protocol contains provisions for parties to "determine the feasibility of banning or restricting imports from non-parties or products produced with but not containing controlled substances". However, these restrictions are part of a multilateral environmental agreement. These trade measures have not been implemented. If they were, however, and if a complaint was made to the WTO, it is not obvious how a panel would rule in this case, or what changes such a ruling would bring about, given that a large number of WTO members are also parties to the Montreal Protocol.

Implementation strategy of environmental taxes

How should environmental taxes be implemented? There are compelling reasons for wanting to introduce taxes gradually, both for domestic and international reasons. The European Commission, in its proposal to adopt a carbon/energy tax, recognised this (EC, 1991): "In order to ensure a smooth introduction of the increased energy prices which will result from such a tax and to reduce the overall cost effect to consumers and industry, an early announcement and a gradual introduction is essential."

The reason for phasing in taxes is to reduce adjustment costs. However, policy makers should also explain the reasons for implementing the tax, and indicate how the tax might change over time. Just as important as the task of reducing adjustment costs is that of coordinating expectations about the policy. The effectiveness of the tax will not depend only on its current level; it will also depend on expectations about its persistence and future levels. Investment will be driven at least as much by expectations as by the existing level of the tax.

Furthermore, even where the tax is unilateral and intended to address a local environmental problem, representatives of the trade community and the WTO should be consulted where the tax is to be accompanied by a border tax adjustment. Coordination of expectations is as important for international relations as for commercial investment. Such consultation should consider the objectives of the tax as well as its design, with a possible view to exploring alternative policies that would be of less concern to trade.

3.6. Conclusions

There are many variables influencing the trade impact of environmental taxes and competitiveness of industry, and no clear-cut prediction about the impact on trade flows and trade volumes can be made. The trade and investment impacts of environmental regulation which have been measured empirically are almost negligible. Some simulation studies predict strong effects only for a few sectors of the economy. In fact, most existing environmental taxes seem to be too low to induce discernible international impacts. Simulation studies concern hypothetical high carbon energy taxes, currently not in existence.

A clear distinction must be made between short term effects and longer term restructuring effects. In the longer term, environmental taxes should lead to a more efficient structure of the economy both domestically and internationally, and thus lead to smaller trade effects than in the short term. However, competitiveness could be harmed if very substantial environmental taxes on industry are adopted and no offsetting border adjustments are undertaken. In the case of transboundary environmental problems, such potential losses in competitiveness may be accompanied by leakage and reduce the effectiveness of the tax. Hence, failure to make some adjustments may also affect the effectiveness of policy intended to correct for international externalities.

One way to reduce the effects of environmental taxes on competitiveness is to differentiate such taxes by sector. In an extreme form, such differentiation might involve exempting export-oriented industries from paying any tax. This obviously means that pollution that arises from the export sector will not be reduced. The literature indicates that sectoral differentiation is only potentially desirable in a second-best sense. Further, there is some evidence that sectoral differentiation may not work as intended. Since the environmental taxes are imposed in order to induce a reallocation of the economy away from the polluting towards the less polluting activities, one can expect that the polluting industries will need to shrink or need to introduce abatement measures. This internal reallocation will necessarily be accompanied by a restructuring of trade between economies. Consequently, policies which mitigate the trade and investment effects of environmental taxes, will partly prevent the sectoral and technological restructuring of the economy, as such they will forgo the efficiency gains provided by the international division of labour.

Border tax adjustments can potentially neutralise the effects of an environmental tax on competitiveness. Such adjustments appear to pose no problems for the trading system when applied to products. However, they do when applied to processes and production methods (PPMs). The rules for applying border tax adjustments to taxes on processes and process inputs need to be clarified. The issue of border tax adjustments is being addressed by the WTO Committee on Trade and Environment.

Even more important however, is the potential impact of BTAs on the effectiveness of environment taxes, particularly when applied to production processes and methods. Further research in this area is clearly needed. Moreover, the practical aspects or feasibility of applying border tax adjustments for taxes imposed on PPMs also need to be clarified.

Implementation of environmental taxes should state clearly the objectives of the policy and where possible give a clear indication of the evolution of these taxes over time. The effect of the tax will depend not just on its current level but also on expectations about its future level. It is also important that both the domestic and international trade policy community be consulted before environmental taxes which may have significant effects on trade are implemented. Most importantly, in the case of international externalities, policies should be developed within a co-operative multilateral framework.

Notes

1. However, the spread of technology will mitigate the improvement of the competitive position of the firm or industry.

2. Domestic production may remain unchanged but in any case domestic producers will find themselves in a weakened position because of the loss or rather reduction of their home market.

3. This finding, though possible, seems unlikely, at least for relatively small carbon taxes. As noted earlier, studies examining the location decisions of firms have not found that environmental regulations play a dramatic role. See Lucas, Wheeler and Hettige (1992), Low and Yeats (1992), and Grossman and Kreuger (1992).

References

ANDERSON, Kym (1992), "The Standard Welfare Economics of Policies Affecting Trade and the Environment", in Kym Anderson and Richard Blackhurst (eds.) (1992), *The Greening of World Trade Issues*, Harvester Wheatsheaf, Ann Arbor.

ANDERSON, Kym and Richard BLACKHURST (eds.) (1992), *The Greening of World Trade Issues*, Harvester Wheatsheaf, Ann Arbor.

BALDWIN, Robert (1970), *Nontariff Distortions of International Trade*, The Brookings Institution, Washington DC.

BARRETT, Scott (1992), *Strategic Environmental Policy and International Trade*, CSERGE Working Paper GEC 92-19, Norwich.

BURNIAUX, Jean-Marc, John P. MARTIN, Giuseppe NICOLETTI, Joaquim OLIVEIRA MARTINS (1992), *GREEN – A Multi-Sector, Multi-Region General Equilibrium Model for Quantifying the Costs of Curbing CO_2 Emissions: A technical Manual.* Economics Department Working Papers No. 116, OECD, Paris.

BURNIAUX, Jean-Marc, John P. MARTIN, Giuseppe NICOLETTI, Joaquim OLIVEIRA MARTINS (1992a), *The Costs of Reducing CO_2 Emissions: Evidence from GREEN.* Economics Department Working Papers No. 115, OECD, Paris.

CHAPMAN, Duane (1991), "Environmental Standards and International Trade in Automobiles and Copper: The case for a Social Tariff", *Natural Resources Journal*, Vol. 31, No. 3, pp. 449-461.

DEAN, Judith M. (1992), "Trade and the Environment: A Survey of the Literature". In Patrick Low (ed.), *International Trade and the Environment*, World Bank Discussion Papers, No. 159, The World Bank, Washington, DC.

DÉMARET, P. and R. STEWARDSON, "Border Tax Adjustments under GATT and EC Law and General Implications for Environmental Taxes", *Journal of World Trade*, Vol. 28, Nr. 4, pp. 5-65.

FELDER, Stefan and Thomas F. RUTHERFORD (1993), "Unilateral CO_2 Reductions and Carbon Leakage: The Consequences of International Trade in Oil and Basic Materials", *Journal of Environmental Economics and Management*, Vol. 25, Nr. 2, pp. 162-176.

GROSSMAN, Gene M. and Alan B. KRUEGER (1991), *Environmental Impacts of a North American Free Trade Agreement*, Discussion Paper #158, Discussion Papers in Economics, Woodrow Wilson School of Public Affairs and International Affairs, Princeton University, Princeton NJ.

HELPMAN, Elhanan and Paul R. KRUGMAN (1986), *Market Structure and Foreign Trade*, MIT Press, Cambridge Mass.

HETTIGE, Hemamala, Robert E.B. LUCAS, and David WHEELER (1992), "The Toxic Intensity of Industrial Production: Global Patterns, Trends, and Trade Policy", *American Economic Review*, Vol. 82, No. 2, pp. 478-481.

KLEPPER, Gernot and Peter MICHAELIS (1992), *Reducing Cadmium Emissions into the Air*, Kiel Working Paper No. 531, The Kiel Institute of World Economics, Kiel.

LOW, Patrick (ed.) (1992), *International Trade and the Environment*, World Bank Discussion Papers, No. 159, The World Bank, Washington, DC.

LOW, Patrick (1992a), "Trade Measures and Environmental Quality: The Implications for Mexico's Exports". In Patrick Low (ed.) *International Trade and the Environment*. World Bank Discussion Papers, No. 159, The World Bank, Washington, DC.

LUCAS, Robert E.B., David WHEELER, Hemamala HETTIGE (1992), *Economic Development, Environmental Regulation and the International Migration of Toxic Industrial Pollution: 1960-1988,* Policy Research Working Papers, WPS 1062, The World Bank, Washington DC.

LUDEMA, Rodney D. and Ian WOOTON (1992), *Cross-Border Externalities and Trade Liberalization*, Department of Economics, University of Western Ontario, Canada, Manuscript.

MARKUSEN, James R., Edward R MOREY, and Nancy OLEWILER (1991), *Environmental Policy when Market Structure and Plant Locations are Endogenous*, National Bureau of Economic Research Working Paper No. 3671.

MERRIFIELD, John D. (1988), "The Impact of Selected Abatement Strategies on Transnational Pollution, the Terms of Trade, and Factor Rewards: A General Equilibrium Approach", *Journal of Environmental Economics and Management*, Vol. 15.

NICOLETTI, Giuseppe and Joaquim OLIVEIRA-MARTINS (1992), *Global Effects of the European Carbon Tax*, OECD Economics Department Working Papers No. 125, Paris.

OECD (1989), *Economic Instruments for Environmental Protection*, OECD, Paris.

OECD (1991), *Environmental Policy: How to Apply Economic Instruments*, OECD, Paris.

OECD (1993), *Taxation and the Environment: Complementary Policies*, OECD, Paris.

OECD (1993a), *Environmental Policies and Industrial Competitiveness,* OECD, Paris.

OECD (1994), *Managing the Environment: The Role of Economic Instruments,* OECD, Paris.

OECD(1995a), *Global Warming: Economic Dimensions and Policy Responses*, OECD, Paris,

OECD(1995b), *Report on Trade and Environment to the OECD Council at Ministerial Level*, OECD, Paris.

OLIVEIRA-MARTINS, Joaquim, Jean-Marc BURNIAUX, and John P. MARTIN (1992), "Trade and the Effectiveness of Unilat eral CO_2-Abatement Policies: Evidence from Green", *OECD Economic Studies*, No. 19, Paris.

OLIVEIRA-MARTINS, Joaquim, Jean-Marc BURNIAUX, John P. MARTIN, Giuseppe NICOLETTI (1992a), *The Costs o Reducing CO_2 Emissions: A Comparison of Carbon Tax Curves with GREEN.* Economics Department Working Paper No. 118, OECD, Paris.

PERRONI, Carlo and Thomas F. RUTHERFORD (1993), "International Trade in Carbon Emission Rights and Basic Materials General Equilibrium Calculations for 2020", *Scandinavian Journal of Economics,* Vol. 95, No. 3, pp. 257-278.

PEZZEY, John (1991), *Impacts of Greenhouse Gas Control Strategies on UK Competitiveness*, Department of Trade and Industry London.

RAUSCHER, Michael (1993), *Environmental Regulation and International Capital Allocation*, Nota di Lavoro 79.93, Fondazion Eni Enrico Mattei, Milano.

ROBISON, H. David (1988), "Industrial Pollution Abatement: The Impact on Balance of Trade", *Canadian Journal of Economic* Vol. 21, No. 1, pp. 187-199.

SORENSEN, Peter Birch (1993), "Pollution Taxes and International Competitiveness: Some Selected Policy Issues", In OECD *Environmental Policies and Industrial Competitiveness*, Paris, pp. 63-68.

SYMONS, E.J., John L.R. PROOPS, P.W. GAY (1990), *Carbon Taxes, Consumer Demand and Carbon Dioxide Emission: A Simulation Analysis for the UK*, Department of Economics and Management Science, University of Keele.

TOBEY, James A. (1990), "The Effects of Domestic Environmental Policies on Patterns of World Trade: An Empirical Test" *Kyklos*, Vol. 43, No. 2.

ULPH, Alistair (1993), *Environmental Policy, Plant Location and Government Protection*, Nota di Lavoro 43.93, Fondazione En Enrico Mattei, Milano.

ULPH, David (1993), *Strategic Innovation and Strategic Environmental Policy*, Nota di Lavoro 42.93, Fondazione Eni Enrico Mattei, Milano.

WHALLEY, John and Randall WIGLE (1991), "The international Incidence of Carbon Taxes", in R. Dornbusch and J. Poterba (eds.), *Economic Policy Responses to Global Warming*, MIT Press, Cambridge MA.

WHEELER, David and Paul MARTIN (1992), "Prices, Policies, and the International Diffusion of Clean Technology: The case o Wood Pulp Production", In: Patrick Low (ed.), *International Trade and the Environment,* World Bank Discussion Papers No. 159, The World Bank, Washington, DC.

WIEßNER, Elke (1991), *Umwelt und Außenhandel*, Nomos Verlagsgesellschaft, Baden-Baden.

WINTER, L. Alan (1992), "The Trade and Welfare Effects of Greenhouse Gas Abatement: A Survey of Empirical Estimates", in Kym Anderson and Richard Blackhurst (eds.) (1992), *The Greening of World Trade Issues*, Harvester Wheatsheaf, Ann Arbor

Chapter 4

DISTRIBUTIONAL EFFECTS OF ENVIRONMENTAL TAXES
AND COMPENSATION MEASURES

4.1. Introduction

Many of the OECD countries that have introduced environmental taxes have found that the distributional effects of these measures have been a major area of political controversy, and have required close attention in policy design and presentation. A feature of some of the policy "packages" which countries have employed to secure public support for environmental tax reforms has been the inclusion of explicit or implicit financial "compensation" to key groups adversely affected by the proposed reform.

This chapter examines the empirical evidence on distributional issues likely to be raised by environmental tax policies. The focus of the chapter is principally on distributional issues arising within OECD countries, in the sense of policy effects which would bear unevenly on different groups within the population (income groups, industries, regions, etc.). There are also important distributional issues between countries which may arise, particularly in the context of global policies on climate change, but these have been discussed extensively in other work, and lie beyond the scope of this chapter.

Following this introduction, the chapter is in three main sections. Section 2 sets out some issues regarding the analytical framework for analysing the distributional effects of environmental taxes. Section 3 then summarises results from existing empirical studies on the distributional effects of environmental taxes. Section 4 discusses possible policy approaches to resolving any distributional problems which environmental taxes might generate. Such measures, aiming to mitigate or compensate for the distributional incidence of ecotaxes, could take a number of forms. These are set out and evaluated, and available empirical evidence summarised.

Whilst distributional issues could arise with a number of environmental taxes, in practice, most of the empirical research and policy attention relates to one particular group of measures, the use of carbon taxes, or other energy taxes, to control greenhouse gas emissions from fossil fuel use. Particularly significant distributional issues arise in this case, due to the significant share of total expenditures which would be covered by the tax,

the role of energy purchases as a "necessity" in household budgets in at least some OECD countries, and the high level of the carbon taxes which some studies have suggested might ultimately be required in order to bring global warming under control.

4.2. Analytical framework

Four key issues arise in defining an appropriate analytical framework for analysing the distributional effects of environmental taxes.

Relevant costs and benefits

Firstly, what costs and benefits should be taken into account in assessing the distributional impact of environmental taxes? Potentially, there may be two general types of distributional effect: long-run distributional shifts, reflecting the nature of the permanent change in the pattern of economic activity that would be the result of using environmental taxes, and "short-run" distributional issues arising during the adjustment process.

The long-run distributional effects include: the distribution of tax payments; the distribution of abatement costs; and the distribution of environmental benefits. Of these, the distribution of the burden of additional tax payments is probably likely to be the most unevenly distributed, and the source of most concern. In the short term, there may be significant adjustment costs to be taken into account, and these may be very unevenly distributed. These could include, for example, lower returns on investment and lower wages or unemployment that might result if environmental taxes led to changes in the competitive position of different industries, or major industrial restructuring. Whilst, in common with other adjustment problems, these costs are a feature of transition, rather than permanent, it is difficult to be precise over the length of time that these adjustment costs would persist, and it is possible that, in some cases, "short-term" adjustment costs could last for some considerable period.

Formal and effective incidence

A second issue concerns the depth of the analysis. Should we be concerned simply with the distribution of initial (or "formal") incidence of environmental tax payments, or with their final incidence (*i.e*, with who bears the ultimate extra financial burden)? In practice both concepts may be relevant; the former may give a good guide to possible political difficulties in policy-making, whilst the latter may be more relevant in assessing the objective distributional impact of policy.

General theoretical conclusions concerning the final incidence of taxes on the sale of goods can provide some insights into how the final incidence of a carbon tax might differ from its formal incidence. The final incidence of taxes on goods will be divided between the buyer and seller according to the price elasticities of demand and supply. The buyer will tend to bear the bulk of the burden of the tax where the supply of the good is relatively elastic and the demand relatively inelastic; where, on the other hand, if supply is relatively inelastic and demand is relatively elastic, the incidence of the tax will be mainly on the seller. In turn, if the tax incidence falls on the seller, the tax burden may be shared among the various factors of production, including capital and resource owners and labour. As a rule it does not matter from the point of view of the final incidence whether it is the buyer or the seller in a particular transaction who is actually responsible for paying the tax.

The baseline for comparison

What is meant by the distributional effects of environmental taxes will depend on what is taken as the baseline for comparison. That is, should this be the no-change baseline where no policy intervention takes place, or should it be the distributional effects of achieving the same environmental improvements through the use of other instruments? The choice of baseline will determine, amongst other things, which of the various costs and benefits are relevant in assessing the distributional incidence of a particular environmental tax measure. For example, if the analysis proceeds from the basis that the relevant alternative to an environmental tax is a less effective environmental policy, then one element which will be relevant in assessing the overall distributional impact of the environmental tax is the distribution of the greater environmental benefits which the policy would achieve.

Relevant distributional dimensions

Various different notions of distribution may be relevant, depending on the instrument being employed and the political context of policy-making.

These could include:
- distribution across income groups, or other measures of relative household living standards;
- distribution between household types, especially between households according to age and household composition;
- distribution between business and households;
- distribution between types of firm, or across industries;
- regional distribution.

Of these, two in particular – the distribution in relation to standards of living, and distribution between business and households – call for some discussion, and are considered in the sections below.

i) Distribution across households at different standards of living

The standards of living of different households may be measured in a number of different ways. Some measures used in distributional analyses include:
- Gross household income. Whilst straightforward, this has the drawback that large households with many earners tend to be counted as well-off, disregarding the fact that they also have larger numbers of individual members to support.
- Household "equivalent income". Total household income is adjusted to reflect the number of household members.
- Household total expenditure. This may be a better measure than current income of the long-term standard of living of households, since it may smooth out some of the effects of temporary fluctuations in household incomes (due to unexpected income windfalls, temporary unemployment or sickness, etc.). This approach has been used in a number of recent studies. For example, Poterba (1991) shows that a carbon tax is found to be less regressive using expenditure as the measure of household living standards, than it appears when distributional incidence is based on current income.

The choice between income and expenditure to assess distributional incidence remains controversial. It should be observed, however, that in assessing policy changes, both current incomes and expenditures may be relevant, especially in assessing the impact of a policy change on current generations. Thus, for example, the present generation of old age pensioners would be more adversely affected by new taxes on expenditures than on incomes, even if subsequent generations would pay the same lifetime tax bill under each.

ii) Distribution between business and households

An issue which often arises as a matter of policy concern is the possibility that an environmental tax might alter the balance of tax payments between "business" and "household" taxpayers. Some environmental taxes might be levied wholly, or substantially, on business inputs or outputs, and these might be seen as increasing the relative tax burden on business, compared to the burden borne by households.

In terms of final incidence, the notion of a tax burden which is borne by business is difficult to sustain. Ultimately, taxes levied on businesses are borne by individuals, either in their role as shareholders of the business, as customers, or as employees. The burden of an environmental tax levied on polluting emissions by a business would, on this view, ultimately have to be borne by one or more of:

- customers of the firm's output, if the environmental tax payment or the costs of abatement measures were passed on in higher prices;
- shareholders of the firm, if the additional tax payment or costs of abatement measures led to reduced profits;
- employees of the firm, if competitive pressures from firms in other areas, not subject to the tax, led to lower wage rates paid to the firm's employees.

Distributional issues could still, of course occur, in the sense that the final incidence of an environmental tax might be unevenly distributed, and might fall particularly heavily on groups of households of particular concern. However, the concern would then relate to the dimensions of the household distribution set out above, rather than to the balance between business and household taxpayers, as an issue of specific concern in its own right.

Nevertheless, concerns about the balance of taxation between business and household taxpayers are a matter of practical interest amongst politicians and policy-makers in a number of countries. For example, in the Netherlands, explicit undertakings have in the past been made about the balance between these two groups of taxpayer, and environmental taxes would have to be introduced in the context of a package which left the overall balance of taxes contributed by business and household taxpayers unchanged.

4.3. Empirical evidence and simulation results

Distributional impacts of carbon taxes and other energy taxes

The distributional impact of carbon taxes, or of other energy taxes introduced to curb energy-related emissions, has been a major issue in the policy debate, both in the European countries that have introduced carbon taxes, and in the European Union and the United States where proposals for major new taxes on energy have encountered strong political opposition. The distributional issues relate both to the additional taxes on direct household purchases of energy (household energy consumption for heating, lighting, etc., and household purchases of motor fuel), and also possible distributional

effects arising from the extra taxation of households' indirect energy use, through the taxation of energy used in the production of goods which households purchase.

A key issue, not always made explicit in the literature, concerns the incidence of the tax – *i.e.* where the ultimate burden of the carbon tax falls. Would a carbon tax be passed on in higher prices for fuels and products manufactured using energy, or would it be passed back, for example to the owners of energy resources in the form of lower pre-tax prices for energy, or to various other factors of production? The extent to which the tax is passed on in prices will depend, in part, on the international context in which a carbon tax is introduced. If other countries also implement similar measures, it is more likely that some of the burden of the tax will be borne by the owners of energy resources, rather than by energy consumers.

Distributional effects of taxes on household energy use

Poterba (1991), using US data from the 1985-86 Consumer Expenditure Survey, estimates that a carbon tax would have a regressive incidence, regardless of whether income or expenditure is used to measure relative living standards. However, the carbon tax appears much more regressive if income is used than if expenditure is used.

On the income basis, the carbon tax appears sharply regressive. The per centage burden of the additional tax falls sharply with increasing income; for the poorest decile the additional tax burden would be equivalent to 10.1 per cent of income, for the second decile 5 per cent, and for the top decile, 1.5 per cent. On the other hand, using *expenditure* deciles and expenditures the denominator in calculating the per centage burden shows a much less regressive profile: the bottom decile pays additional tax equivalent to 3.7 per cent of spending whilst the top decile pays an additional 2.3 per cent of spending. Poterba expresses a clear preference for the latter basis of calculation, which he argues is more consistent with a life-cycle concept of income than the use of current income. On the basis of his preferred definition, the regressivity of the carbon tax appears quite modest.

These estimates of the distributional incidence of a carbon tax in the United States made by Poterba may be compared to the results for six European Union countries calculated by Pearson and Smith (1991) using published tables of 1985 Eurostat data. In five of the six countries, the burden of carbon tax payments is only weakly related to income, if at all. Only in Ireland is there evidence of a significantly regressive pattern to household carbon tax payments. A more detailed analysis of the distributional incidence of the EU's proposed carbon tax in Ireland by Scott (1992) confirms that it would be significantly regressive; whilst the average household tax payment would be 1.5 per cent of household spending, the tax payment of the bottom decile would be 2.7 per cent of spending, and the payment of the top decile 1.0 per cent.

Box 4.1. EMPIRICAL AND SIMULATION METHODS

To the extent that environmental taxes fall directly on goods purchased by households for final consumption, their distributional impact may be inferred from data on the expenditure patterns of households. In some studies, the existing pattern of spending is used to estimate the distributional impact of environmental taxes levied on particular goods; in other studies, simulation models are used to take account of possible change in the pattern of household spending in response to the change in taxation.

Analysing the distributional effects on households of environmental taxes imposed on industrial inputs is considerably more complex than assessing the effects of environmental taxes on consumer spending, for two important reasons. One is that there is a need to link industrial input taxes to individual households, through changes in prices and incomes. The other is that there is a much greater likelihood that macroeconomic effects or other system-wide repercussions will be significant, and there is therefore a need to take these into account in the analysis.

Approaches which have been used to assess the impact of taxes on industrial inputs include the use of input-output models to trace input taxes through to the prices of goods and services purchased by households. These models reflect the rather strong assumption that the relationship between inputs and outputs in production is unaffected by changes in input prices; in other words, that there is no possibility for substitution between inputs. This is only likely to be a good reflection of actual behavioural responses in the short term, when firms are operating with a given capital stock.

In order to go beyond the simple "fixed-coefficients" assumption (zero factor substitution) of input-output analysis, rather more extensive information is needed about the relevant elasticities of supply, demand and substitution. Since the adjustment processes involved would be likely to have extensive implications, for the level and pattern of activity of particular sectors, of prices, and of incomes, more extensive studies of the effects of taxes on industrial inputs have generally been conducted within the framework provided by a model of the overall economy, either in the form of a short or medium-run macroeconomic model, or a computable general equilibrium model. Whilst such models are generally designed for looking at changes in economy-wide aggregates rather than at distributional questions, it is possible to integrate the output from such models with a distributional model, so as to look at the effects of relative price changes, and changes in incomes and activity, on different groups in the population.

The above studies have taken the pattern of household energy consumption as given, and unaffected by the change in energy taxes and prices. Pearson and Smith (1991) report an analysis of the distributional incidence of the EC's proposed carbon/energy tax in the United Kingdom, in which account is taken of the changes in household spending induced by the tax. Overall, they show that the estimated pattern of additional taxation is very close to that which would be estimated on the basis of unchanged consumption patterns. However, they show that there are significantly larger adjustments in energy consumption by poorer households than by other households. A carbon tax at a level equivalent to $10 per barrel would lead to an overall reduction of some 6.5 per cent in domestic energy consumption (in volume terms), but a reduction of nearly 10 per cent in the energy consumption of the poorest 20 per cent of households. To the extent that the changes in consumption reflect costs imposed on households, these costs should be reflected in the distributional impact of the carbon tax.

Distributional effects of taxes on industrial energy use

In addition to the direct distributional effects working through the prices of household purchases of domestic energy and motor fuels, a carbon tax applied to all fuels would have a number of indirect distributional effects, as a result of the taxes imposed on industrial purchases of energy.

Input-output analysis has been used by Casler and Rafiqui (1993) and Symons, Proops and Gay (1994) to calculate the distributional impact of higher taxes on energy inputs, assuming the tax is fully passed on to consumers and that no change takes place to the pattern of inputs used in production. These assumptions are of course strong, and probably only a reasonable approximation in the short-term. Over a longer time period, the assumption of no factor substitution in production is clearly restrictive; it does not allow for any effect of the tax on carbon emissions per unit of production. However, despite the limitations of the method, it nonetheless may provide a reasonably straightforward source of information on the first-round distributional effects of environmental taxes on industrial inputs.

Casler and Rafiqui (1993) use 1985 input-output data and consumer expenditure survey data for the United States to assess the direct and indirect energy input to household consumption, and its distribution across income groups and across other consumer classifications, including age categories and rural/urban areas. Relative to the expenditure share of the highest income quintile, households in lower income quintiles were found to have a higher expenditure share on direct energy purchases, and also a higher total (direct plus indirect) energy share. This latter result is indicated by the total energy content (Btu) per dollar of expenditure, which was estimated to be about 8 per cent higher for the poorest quintile than for the richest quintile (Table 4.1). In urban areas, direct expenditure shares on energy were found, on average, to be less than 80 per cent of the direct energy shares of rural households (within this total, gasoline shares of urban households were less than 75 per cent of gasoline shares of rural households), and total direct and indirect energy per dollar of expenditure by urban households was 87 per cent of total energy per dollar spent by rural households. Across age groups,[1] both direct and total energy shares peaked amongst the 55-64 age group; direct energy shares were smaller amongst the under-35 age groups than amongst the 65-74 age group, whilst total energy shares were somewhat higher amongst the under-35 group than amongst the 65-74 group.

Symons, Proops and Gay (1994) present estimates of the effects on consumer prices of a carbon tax at various levels, based on the 1984 UK Input-Output tables, assuming the higher energy input prices would be fully passed on at subsequent stages. The largest increases in relative prices would be in the prices of domestic energy and petrol, but appreciable price effects might also be felt in the prices of some other commodities. Some of the increase in aggregate prices could be eliminated if the revenue were used to reduce other indirect taxes. These estimates are then fed into a consumer spending microsimulation model to derive effects on

household tax payments (grouping households by expenditure deciles), and various measures of household inequality.

The authors explore a number of possible policy packages, four of which are summarised in Table 4.2. The first scenario is simply the use of a high carbon tax, sufficient to achieve the Toronto target for emissions reduction in the UK through changes in the pattern of sectoral activity.[2] Scenario 2 achieves the same emissions reduction, through a package which levies a higher carbon tax than Scenario 1, whilst at the same time reducing petrol excise taxes, so that the price of petrol remains unchanged. Scenario 3 has the same level of energy and petrol excises, but uses some of the revenue raised to abolish VAT; the emissions reduction achieved is about three quarters that achieved in the first two scenarios. Scenario 4 uses some of the revenue to make sharp increases in the rates of social transfer payments, instead of reducing VAT; a lower emissions reduction is achieved than in any of the other scenarios.

Symons, Proops and Gay show that the carbon tax would have a significantly adverse effect on the incomes of poorer households, and on household inequality (as measured by Atkinson inequality indices and the Gini coefficient), except in the case where a substantial proportion of the revenues is used to increase social transfer payments. The results indicate the sensitivity of estimates of distributional effects to the precise content of the package of accompanying measures. In particular, it can be seen that the package in which revenue is used to reduce VAT involves a rise in inequality, even in comparison to the scenarios in which compensation is not paid.

Unless all of the burden of a carbon tax on energy inputs can be passed on in higher prices, without any change in the pattern of consumers' expenditure, at least some of the burden of the tax will be borne by the owners of the different factors of production, including capital, labour and natural resources, especially energy resources. One obvious possibility is that at least part of the carbon tax on energy will be borne by the owners of reserves of carbon-based energy sources, as a result of lower pre-tax prices for carbon-based energy, and the profitability of

Table 4.1. **Direct and indirect energy inputs to household consumption, by income group, United States**

1985

		Quintile of household income				
	All households	Poorest	2	3	4	Richest
Direct energy expenditure, as share of total spending	9.512	10.709	10.987	10.340	9.926	7.914
Ratio of direct to indirect energy expenditure	0.290	0.321	0.325	0.309	0.296	0.252
Total energy content (Btu) per dollar of expenditure (index, all households = 100)	100	101.8	104.7	103.7	102.4	94.5

Source: Casler and Rafiqui (1993).

Table 4.2. **Carbon tax scenarios: simulated effects of policy packages including compensation measures, United Kingdom**

1990 basis

	Scenario 1 Carbon tax £240/tonne	Scenario 2 Carbon tax £278/tonne; petrol excise halved	Scenario 3 Carbon tax £278/tonne; petrol excise halved; VAT reduced	Scenario 4 Carbon tax £278/tonne; petrol excise halved; benefits reform
CO_2 reduction achieved %	19.7	19.6	14.1	11.3
Percentage price changes for goods with high-CO_2 intensity				
Household energy	79.0	91.2	91.2	91.2
Petrol	34.7	–0.5	–13.5	–0.5
Durables, china	8.5	9.8	–4.5	9.8
Transport	5.2	6.1	0.3	6.1
Food	2.9	3.4	–0.3	3.4
Percentage increase in government indirect tax revenue	47.7	47.1	–1.2	2.9
Change in average disposable expenditure				
All households	–13%	–12%	–8%	+5%
Bottom decile	–17%	–18%	–14%	+56%
Atkinson inequality indices				
Inequality aversion = 0.1 (pre-reform = 0.026)	0.027	0.028	0.029	0.023
Inequality aversion =1 (pre-reform = 0.264)	0.282	0.286	0.296	0.220
Inequality aversion = 10 (pre-reform = 0.853)	0.879	0.883	0.888	0.740
Gini coefficient (pre-reform = 0.386)	0.397	0.400	0.406	0.362

Source: Symons, Proops and Gay (1994).

existing extraction activities may fall. Changes in the profitability of extraction activities will affect the real incomes and wealth of the households owning shares in resource extraction businesses. The profitability of other firms may change too, especially if consumer demand switches away from energy-intensive goods and services, and this may affect the profits received by their owners, and the wages and employment prospects of their employees. Depending on the complementarity or substitutability of different factors in production, effects could be felt on the return to capital and labour even outside the sectors directly affected.

To quantify the full range of effects set out above would require a comprehensive general equilibrium model, based on detailed information about consumer demands, and the substitutability of different factors in production. Many of the key behavioural and technical parameters are unknown, and those estimates that do exist are often subject to a wide margin of error.

Schillo *et al* (1992) simulate the overall distributional incidence of a carbon tax in the United States, taking into account both direct and indirect effects, and incorporating a range of system-wide economic repercussions. Three distributional analyses are presented, each of which is based on a two-stage simulation, in which a simulation is initially made of the effects of a carbon on aggregate, macroeconomic, variables, and this is then fed

into a desegregated analysis of how this overall change in incomes, prices and taxes would result in distributional effects on households or household types.

Three main channels by which distributional effects can arise are distinguished in the study. First, there are price effects, through the differential impact of price changes on different groups. Second, there are income effects, arising principally through changes in the rate and pattern of economic growth, and the differential impact of these income changes on different groups in the population. Third, there are tax effects, arising through the reductions in other taxes which can be made, as a result of the revenues being raised from the carbon tax. A number of different options are studied for possible schemes of tax reduction (a revenue-neutral lump sum rebate per adult, an equal proportionate reduction in the rates of income tax, and a combined reduction in marginal tax rates on both labour and capital), and the study shows that which option is chosen has an appreciable bearing on the final distributional outcome.

Two of the distributional analyses use DRI's macroeconomic model as the first stage in the simulation, to show how aggregate variables would adjust over the short-to-medium term (up to 2010), to the introduction of a carbon tax. When the macro forecasts of relative price changes, income changes, and tax changes are fed into DRI's CES/DECO distributional model, this shows a complex pattern of distributional effects. In broad terms, with revenue neutrality achieved either through a lump-sum rebate or a personal income tax reduction, the overall effect would be regressive; the real incomes of the bottom quintile would fall by about 0.5 per cent compared to the baseline with the lump-rum rebate, and 1.5 per cent with the income tax reduction, whilst the incomes of higher income groups would be broadly unaffected. On the other hand, when revenues are returned through reductions in taxes on both capital and labour, the distributional impact would be considerably less regressive; indeed, by 2010, the incomes of the bottom two quintiles would be higher than in the base case, whilst the incomes of the top three quintiles would fall. Much of this effect arises through reductions in prices, which are particularly concentrated on commodities which are a large part of the spending of poorer households.

The DRI macrosimulation results are also fed into the Urban Institute's TRIM2 microsimulation model, which is based on individual and household data for a sample of some 60,000 households from the Current Population Survey, and a detailed representation of household tax payments and transfer entitlements. If carbon tax revenues are returned through reductions in personal income tax rates, the induced income changes lead to increase in the pre-tax cash incomes of the bottom four deciles of the income distribution. On average across all households, however, pre-tax cash incomes fall, in nominal terms, by 0.26 per cent. Overall post-tax incomes would be some 0.06 per cent higher, and all but the top 5 per cent of the income distribution would experience rises in post-tax nominal incomes. Since, however, the overall price level is higher, real post tax incomes fall throughout the income distribution, although the fall is somewhat less for the bottom two deciles than for the average of all households.

The third distributional analysis uses the Jorgenson/Wilcoxen computable general equilibrium model to generate aggregate changes in macroeconomic variables, and then feeds these results into the Jorgenson/Slesnick/Wilcoxen distributional model. In contrast to the short-to-medium term focus of the DRI macro model, the Jorgenson/Wilcoxen aggregate analysis represents a long-run, neoclassical, process of adjustment of product and factor markets, in which commodity and factor prices adjust to new equilibrium levels. Also, the distributional analysis differs, taking the form of an analysis of changes in lifetime welfare of different household types (''dynasties'').

In terms of the distributional effects across households with different levels of wealth, J/S/W find very little wealth-related variation. With a lump-sum redistribution of revenues, the effect of the carbon tax on dynasties with mean wealth, half mean wealth and twice mean wealth is, in each case, to reduce wealth by about 1 per cent. When the revenue is used to reduce labour taxes, the wealth of each of these three groups rises, by about 0.6 per cent for average wealth, 0.5 per cent for half

average and 0.7 per cent for twice-average. Similar, though slightly lower, results are obtained where revenue is used to reduce both labour and capital taxes. Where capital taxes alone are reduced, none of the three wealth groups experiences any significant change in aggregate wealth from the base case.

An important observation to be made about the J/S/W analysis is that the notion of distributional effects is rather different to that in nearly all of the other studies discussed in this chapter. Since the focus of J/S/W is on lifetime wealth effects, on household dynasties, they do not capture many of the distributional issues which may be of concern to policy-makers, such as the possibility of distributional shifts between present and future generations. Thus, whilst a carbon tax might have a broadly neutral effect on lifetime wealth, introduction of a carbon tax could lead to significant losses for the current generation of poor, elderly households. These effects are different from those addressed in the analysis of distributional effects among household dynasties.

Distributional implications of other taxes

In comparison with the extensive attention which has been paid to carbon and energy taxes, much less empirical evidence exists on the distributional effects of other possible environmental taxes. There may be a number of reasons for this. In general these would relate to less significant components of household spending, with less of a clear-cut ''necessity'' status, and the impact on the tax payments of individual households would be much lower, and perhaps also less regressive.

In the United States there has been concern that additional *taxes on motor fuels* could be regressively-distributed. Table 4.3 summarises results from a Congressional Budget Office study of the distributional incidence of excise taxes, which show a regressive incidence of motor fuel taxes in relation to household income. However, as the CBO figures show, and as Poterba (1989) has discussed, the pattern of motor fuel taxes looks less regressive if tax burdens are calculated using household total expenditures rather than incomes.

It appears, however, that this conclusion would not hold across the entire OECD area. In the United Kingdom, according to Johnson, McKay and Smith (1990), higher petrol taxes would appear to be broadly progressively-distributed across income groups.

Different patterns of motor fuel consumption among different countries and different areas within countries may partly reflect the availability of good substitutes for private motoring. In European cities, where good-quality public transport is widely available, the use of a private car is not a necessity for individuals commuting to work, or making many other journeys. This may be less true in many cities in the United States. In addition, within European countries, there is a clear difference between urban and rural areas in the extent to which public transport

Table 4.3. **Distributional impact of a motor fuel tax increase in the United States, by adjusted post-tax income quintiles, age of family head, and region, 1990**

	Net tax increase (dollars)	Net tax increase (percentage of post-tax income)	Net tax increase (percentage of total expenditures)
Post tax family income			
Bottom quintile	99	1.2	0.5
2nd quintile	127	0.7	0.5
3rd quintile	158	0.6	0.5
4th quintile	187	0.5	0.5
Top quintile	223	0.3	0.4
Age of family head			
Under 30	140	0.6	0.5
30-44	180	0.5	0.5
45-59	200	0.5	0.5
60-74	141	0.4	0.5
75 and over	77	0.3	0.4
Region			
Northeast	151	0.4	0.4
Midwest	159	0.5	0.5
South	164	0.5	0.5
West	173	0.5	0.4
Rural	164	0.6	0.6
All families	162	0.5	0.5

Source: Congressional Budget Office (1990).

provides a close substitute for private car use. These differences may have implications for the distributional impact of higher excise taxes on motoring. Even where higher motor fuel taxes would have a progressive distributional incidence across the population as a whole, there may be concerns about the impact on low-income individuals in rural areas.

Distributional issues also arise where environmental policies might involve a move away from tax-financed provision of certain services, to the use of *charges* related to the amounts consumed or used by individual households. Such reforms might include financing garbage collection, or household water and sewerage services, through charges based on use rather than through existing taxes.

For the United Kingdom, Rajah and Smith (1993) look at the distributional implications of a move from the existing system of household charges for water and sewerage services, which involve quasi-taxes, levied on a property tax base, to charging based on metered water consumption. They show that a switch to water metering would have a very similar distributional incidence across income groups to the incidence of the existing quasi-tax system of finance known as "water rates". However, there would be a distinct pattern of gainers and losers across household types as a result of the introduction of universal water metering. As a result of the strong correlation between household size and water consumption, large households would tend to lose whereas smaller households tend to gain.

4.4. Policy implications

As OECD (1994) observes, it is almost inevitable that the use of economic instruments such as environmental taxes will create losers as well as winners. The losers will include any individuals put out of work during the transition to the new policy. In addition, the long-run costs and benefits of environmental tax measures may be unevenly distributed. Particular concerns relate to the distributional incidence of the additional tax payments, which may, in some cases (such as the case of taxes on domestic energy) bear particularly heavily on poorer households, or on other vulnerable groups.

Action to offset these distributional effects may be justified for two reasons (OECD, 1994; Harrison and Portney, 1982; Burtraw and Portney, 1991).

- There is a pragmatic case for offsetting distributional effects, if those who would otherwise lose might be sufficiently influential or well-organised as to be able to block implementation of the measure.
- There is a normative case for offsetting the distributional effects of environmental taxes, based on objectives of equity or social justice which may underlie public policy. If environmental taxes shift the tax burden significantly towards poorer or more vulnerable groups in society, adjustments may be sought in other areas of policy, to offset all or part of the losses experienced by poor or vulnerable households.

Neither of these arguments necessarily implies any greater case for compensation for the distributional effects of environmental taxes than for other policy measures and reforms. Governments frequently make changes to policy which may have significant distributional effects without introducing parallel compensation measures. There may be good reasons for this:

- A readiness to make compensation to transitional losers from policy changes may expose governments to lobbying pressures for excessive or unjustified compensation; these pressures may be easier to resist if governments maintain a clear commitment not to make compensation in any circumstances.
- Gains and losses from public policy changes may be small relative to the scale of gains and losses which arise from natural adjustment processes in the economy. It may be argued that there is nothing special about losses due to public policy reforms which would justify these being compensated, when other, larger, losses arising from non-policy sources remain uncompensated.
- Equity objectives may be more efficiently achieved if an overall policy is designed, than if a distributional policy accumulates as a result of a sequence of *ad hoc* compensation measures for particular policy measures.

Over and above these more general considerations regarding the merits of compensation, it might be argued that some of the losers from environmental policies have no right to be compensated, in that what environmental policy measures are aiming to do is correct the harm that they have previously been causing society. Whatever the merits of these various arguments, we may note the conclusion of OECD (1994) that "on balance it seems useful to consider methods of compensating those who lose from environmental regulation, or at least to acknowledge that groups who lose will press for compensation... It would seem bad politics to assume that groups adversely affected will not make their concerns known." (OECD, 1994).

This section therefore sets out a range of possible policy strategies for dealing with the social and distributional issues raised within member states by climate change policy measures. Given the conclusions of the previous section that the main distributional issues seem likely to arise in the case of carbon taxes and other large-scale energy tax reforms, most of the discussion concentrates on these cases, although many of the arguments would be more widely applicable.

Mitigation and compensation

OECD (1994) distinguishes between "mitigation" and "compensation" as two alternative strategies for offsetting undesired distributional effects, in the following terms:

"**Mitigation** refers to reducing the impacts of the programme *ex ante* so that the potential impacts do not occur. For example, the government might reduce or eliminate a pollution control requirement because it would harm particular groups.

"**Compensation** refers to aid to particular groups *ex post* so that they are (at least partly) 'made whole'. For example, the government may go ahead with a policy it knows will harm workers in the region, but it will provide income support and training programmes to compensate."

In the context of environmental taxes, mitigation strategies would seem to be more widely considered as a means to limit the transitional costs of implementing energy taxes, than as a way of offsetting the long-run impact which such taxes might have on the distribution of incomes. Some examples of mitigation measures which have been suggested, or implemented, in the context of environmental tax measures include the following:

- The European Commission's initial proposals for an EC carbon/energy tax involved the exemption from the tax of six energy intensive sectors of industry – steel, chemicals, non-ferrous metals, cement, glass, pulp and paper. The rationale for this was that these sectors would suffer extreme adjustment pressures if subject to the carbon/energy tax, in circumstances where major international competitors outside the Community were not subject to similarly-high energy prices. Initially it was suggested that these exemptions would be ended if other major competitors introduced similar tax measures to the EC carbon/energy tax; later versions of the proposal did not include the sectoral exemptions (although there were some other, less extensive, exemption provisions), because it had been decided that the EC tax would not be introduced at all without corresponding measures in other major countries. Extensive international coordination of climate change policies would, of course, be the most effective way of limiting the adjustment pressures experienced by individual countries, and are, as OECD (1994), notes, a major rationale for developing a global comprehensive policy on carbon.
- Similarly, concern about possible adjustment pressures within Europe, between countries reliant on carbon-intensive forms of energy, and countries – such as France – with extensive nuclear power facilities, led the Commission to choose the mixed carbon/energy structure for the tax, rather than a 100 per cent carbon tax. This is consistent with the Community's strategy to reach CO_2 stabilisation through both an improvement in energy efficiency and fuel switching toward energy sources with less or no carbon content.

– The carbon tax introduced in Sweden in 1991 initially limited the impact on high energy users through a ceiling, expressed as a percentage of turnover, on the amount of tax that any business would pay (Bohm, 1991). Subsequent revisions have introduced restrictions on the application of the ceiling provision (from July 1995, the provisions only apply to a handful of companies in the lime and cement industry and only for other fuels than mineral oils). Generally, the burden of the carbon tax on industrial users has been sharply reduced, whilst retaining much higher tax levels on domestic energy users.

Relatively fewer examples can be found of mitigation measures to offset adverse or undesired aspects of the long-term distributional incidence of environmental tax measures. One possible example, common to most countries which have introduced carbon taxes, is the retention of much higher taxes than relative environmental effects would warrant on motor fuels than on domestic energy for heating, lighting and power; such differentiation can, however, equally well be explained in other terms. Another possible measure of this sort might involve the exemption (or lower taxation) of fuels predominantly-used by poorer households. It is clear, however, that the way in which concerns about the long-run distributional impact of environmental taxes on energy and other goods have been reflected in offsetting measures has mainly been through compensation measures of various forms, rather than through adjustments to the initial structure of the tax.

There are, moreover, good reasons for avoiding mitigation wherever possible, and for preferring separate and transparent compensation arrangements. To the extent that mitigation measures adjust the structure of the environmental tax so as to reduce the impact on particular groups, they generally also reduce the effectiveness of the tax in encouraging changes in behaviour by these groups. Thus, for example, the proposed exemptions for energy intensive sectors under the initial version of the European Commission's carbon tax proposal would have meant that these sectors did not face the same financial pressures to reduce energy use and to substitute towards lower-carbon sources of energy as other sectors of industry and as household energy users. As Pearson and Smith (1991) argued, this would have meant that some of the largest energy users would have been immune from the incentive effects of the tax. Higher tax rates would have been required on other sectors to achieve a given reduction in emissions, and the exemption would have distorted the structure of the economy towards energy intensive industries, the opposite of the original objective of the tax.

In comparison to mitigation measures, taking the form of adjustments which are inherent to the structure of the environmental tax, compensation measures are in general better able to offset the various forms of distributional problems which environmental taxes may give rise to. The exception to this would be where compensation was related directly or indirectly to the actual amount of tax paid by individual firms or households. The remaining parts of this section consider the options for compensation in more detail.

Compensation through adjustments to other taxes

Much of the discussion about the distributional effects of environmental taxes considers only the incidence of the environmental tax payments, without considering the use of the revenues that the tax raises. This clearly only addresses one part of the story. The revenues raised from environmental taxes do not simply disappear, but are available for governments to use, either to fund additional spending, or to reduce government borrowing, or to reduce other taxes. This section focuses on the distributional effects of each these revenue uses.

Which of these options governments will choose will of course depend on a range of considerations that are discussed in greater detail in Chapter 5. In many OECD countries, the possibility of increasing the tax burden would appear politically unacceptable, and introducing new environmental taxes would require offsetting reductions in others. "Packaging" environmental taxes together with explicit reductions in other taxes may also be useful as part of the political strategy for implementing environmental taxes (see Chapters 2 and 5). If the distributional impact of environmental taxes is considered in the context of a revenue-neutral policy, it is necessary to specify the form in which the reductions in other taxes would be made since this may have a significant impact on the net distributional effect.

There are two broad approaches which might be taken to using the revenues raised from environmental taxes to reduce other taxes so as to compensate those households losing from the long-run distributional incidence of the taxes:

– reducing taxes which have an offsetting long run distributional incidence. Thus, if the environmental tax has a regressive distributional incidence, other regressive taxes might be reduced correspondingly, so as to leave the overall distributional incidence of the tax system unchanged;
– using tax reductions to stimulate macroeconomic or general equilibrium effects which offset the initial losses suffered as a result of the environmental tax. Thus, if the environmental tax makes poor households worse off, a package of tax measures might be selected which would particularly benefit poor workers and households.

These alternatives are considered in turn.

i) Distributional "rebalancing"

Adjusting the distributional balance of other components of the tax system so as to offset the regressive distributional impact of environmental taxes on energy requires a package of tax reductions to be made to taxes which are, in total, at least as regressive as the environmental tax. Reducing these regressive taxes, or regressive elements of the tax system, will then offset the additional regressivity introduced by the environmental tax, so that the overall distributional impact of the environmental tax reform, taking into account the use of revenues, is at least neutral, if not distributionally progressive.

Where environmental taxes have a regressive distributional incidence because they are levied on an element of household spending – such as energy – which has the demand characteristics of a necessity, household payments of the environmental tax will still be higher amongst households with high incomes than amongst low income households. An equal lump-sum amount – may be in the form of a refundable tax credit – returned to each household, corresponding to the average household environmental tax payment, would be sufficient – indeed, more than sufficient – to offset the regressivity of the environmental tax in these circumstances (Johnson, McKay and Smith, 1990).

Changes to the personal income tax system may also be considered to compensate those most affected by the ecotax. However, caution should be exercised so as not to exacerbate the regressivity of the environmental taxes, say by reducing all existing income tax rates. Increasing income tax thresholds or reducing rates of tax of low incomes would be better alternatives for reducing the regressivity of environmental taxes. However, such policies may not confer any benefit to non-taxpayers, and introducing a refundable income tax credit may be more effective. In turn, given that income tax returns are filled only once a year, a more regular form of compensation would be preferable.

Because sales taxes such as VAT are unlikely to be as regressive as taxes on energy, a reduction in the general sales tax rate is unlikely to be able to fully offset the regressivity of an environmental tax on energy. In comparison to adjustments to income taxes, however, more benefit is likely to accrue to poorer households from reductions in sales taxes, since poor households may pay significant amounts of sales tax on their consumption, whilst being liable for little income tax. A reduction in sales tax rates on other necessities may also be considered but this would create many administrative difficulties and could create inefficiency in the tax system.

In general, however, it may be difficult to adequately compensate poorer households for the regressive burden of environmental taxes on energy by adjustments to the tax system alone. Poor households pay relatively little taxes, and using the tax system to return revenues to poor households will generally return much larger amounts of revenue to better-off households. The tax changes which would be most effective at delivering compensation to poorer households may be undesirable on other grounds – for example, there are strong economic efficiency and tax administration reasons to avoid differentiating the rates of general sales taxes.

It may be possible to target the return of revenues to poorer households much more effectively through adjustments to public transfer systems (social security payments, unemployment insurance payments, pensions, etc.), rather than through the tax system. However, this may distort other market signals, say by reducing the gap between wages from low skilled labour and social benefits (see page 000).

ii) Achieving compensating system-wide gains

An alternative approach to compensation would be to use the revenues from the environmental tax to finance tax reforms which would stimulate income changes which would benefit, in particular, the groups which lose from the environmental tax. These income changes could arise from either macroeconomic or general equilibrium effects of the compensating tax reform measures.

It is possible to think of such channels by which system-wide economic responses to environmental taxes might offset the initial additional tax burden on particular groups. Careful targeting of the use of revenues may achieve particular patterns of economic adjustments which favour the losing groups. For instance, the additional tax revenues from environmental taxes on energy might be used to reduce social security contributions of low income/low skilled labour. Even if some of these macroeconomic effects were not to last indefinitely, the higher level of incomes in the first years of the policy might be seen as sufficient to compensate for the long-run increased tax burden on the groups which lose from the environmental tax.

This type of policy may again be a poor tool to compensate those non-wage earners that are most affected by the environmental tax. Some form of lump-sum compensation or some other measures to improve the energy efficiency of homes may be necessary, and these may be better targeted to those most vulnerable, say the elderly poor.

Other compensation approaches

i) Compensation through changes to the tariff structure for domestic energy supplies

Most utilities supply individual customers according to a tariff structure which includes both "fixed cost" and "variable cost" elements. Thus, for example, typical household bills for electricity or piped gas supply will include both a fixed "connection" cost, unrelated to the amount consumed, and a unit charge levied on each unit used. The unit charges may be a constant amount per unit at all levels of consumption, or may rise or fall as the number of units consumed rises.

From the point of view of environmental policy, externalities associated with energy consumption should be reflected in an increase in the cost of energy consumption at the margin. The distributional problem arises because higher energy taxes increase the cost of marginal consumption by increasing the cost of all units consumed. It might be possible to reduce, or eliminate the distributional problem by measures which increase the marginal cost of consumption, whilst reducing the average cost, either through a reduction in the fixed cost element, or by reducing the price for an initial "allowance" of a given number of units. However, the manipulation of utility tariffs as a means of compensating for environmental taxes on energy would involve a number of significant problems. In particular, requiring utilities to price according to a structure bearing no relationship to underlying supply costs would create new requirements for regulation.

A strategy, which has some practical attractions especially in a system of private utility suppliers, has been suggested in Poterba (1991). This would be to provide a tax credit for energy consumption, up to a certain limit. Consumers might be required to demonstrate their actual level of consumption to the income tax authorities, and would then have their income tax bill reduced by a corresponding amount, up to a given threshold. Of course, the tax credit would be only of benefit to taxpayers, but it would be possible to use a similar system, integrated with the income tax or public transfer systems, for providing payments to non income tax payers. The attraction of these arrangements over other tax or transfer adjustments is that they could target assistance both on particular groups, and in proportion to their consumption, so as to identify within the target groups households or individuals with particularly high energy needs.

ii) The role of energy efficiency policies and market failures

The evidence summarised above has discussed two aspects of the costs to households of adjusting to high environmental taxes on energy – the additional tax burden, and the impact of the tax in reducing household energy consumption. Both of these costs may be greater if energy consumers are prevented by market failures from making optimal adjustments in energy use. An efficient pattern of adjustment to higher energy prices might include both reductions in energy consumption, and also greater levels of investment in various measures to increase the efficiency with which energy is used. In the domestic sector, measures which households can take to improve domestic energy efficiency may include such things as loft insulation, double glazing, and wall insulation. It has been suggested that markets for these investments may be subject to various forms of market failure, possibly including credit market failures, informational

failures, and certain market failures related to housing tenure. Where households are prevented by market failures from adjusting efficiently to higher energy prices, their reductions in energy consumption in response to higher energy prices will tend to be smaller, and more "painful" in terms of their welfare cost.

The social and distributional costs of higher energy prices may be exacerbated if market failures in energy efficiency investment are particularly concentrated amongst low income households, or other vulnerable groups (Smith, 1992). Thus, for example, market failures affecting households at the lower end of the income distribution, such as those related to the credit market, or to housing tenure, may tend to amplify the distributional cost of reducing energy consumption through pricing instruments. Measures to rectify the underlying market failures would then have the twin merits that they would tend to reduce the aggregate economic cost of achieving a given reduction in consumption, and at the same time would also help to reduce the social and distributional cost of higher energy taxation.

Policy measures to correct the market failures which prevent households from adjusting efficiently to higher energy taxes would lead to efficiency gains, and, as observed above, might reduce some of the distributional problems caused by higher environmental taxes on energy. Policies to reduce market failures in energy efficiency affecting the private home rental sector could take a number of forms – including "home energy rating" schemes to improve the quality of information available to private tenants about the likely energy costs of a property, subsidy to the costs incurred by private landlords in installing energy efficiency measures, and direct regulations requiring higher energy efficiency standards in new and/or existing buildings.

The role of adjustment policies

A range of policy measures may be deployed to cope with the adjustment problems resulting from environmental tax measures, and their distributional consequences. One important way in which OECD countries seek to limit the costs borne by individuals when structural changes occur in the economy is through systems of social insurance and unemployment compensation schemes. These act to cushion the fall in the living standard of households suffering income losses during the course of the adjustment process. Such systems face a basic tradeoff between the scale of the compensation they provide (in terms of the proportion of past earnings paid to people who become unemployed), and the maintenance of incentives for the recipients of assistance to seek new employment (which generally requires that assistance levels should be low in relation to the level of pay in alternative occupations).

To the extent that environmental tax measures might lead to a rise in unemployment during the adjustment process, existing systems of social insurance and unemployment compensation can be relied upon to provide a certain offset for the temporary income losses of unemployed individuals. The scale of adjustment required in response to most conceivable ecotax policies is probably modest in relation to past adjustment requirements in OECD countries, although carbon taxes could potentially be levied at very high levels. For example, the adjustment pressures that would be involved in levying a carbon/energy tax at the level proposed by the European Commission would almost certainly be smaller than the adjustment which took place in response to the oil price crises of the 1970s, when a sharp and sudden rise in energy prices led to a large transfer of real incomes to oil producing countries, as well as to industrial and consumer responses to the increased cost of energy. There is no reason to believe that additional enhancement of the systems of social insurance and unemployment compensation in OECD countries would be required to deal with the adjustment requirements of environmental tax policies.

Measures to stimulate replacement employment may in some circumstances be considered. It should be borne in mind that some alternative employment may in any event be provided in industries producing pollution control equipment, where the carbon tax stimulates greater environmental protection investment than would otherwise have been undertaken. However, these new industries may not be located in the same regions, or the same countries, as those adversely affected by climate change policies. Measures to stimulate employment could include supply side interventions, in the form of, for example, retraining policies, to replace obsolete skills, and might also embrace other forms of industrial and technology policy measures. A contribution to ensuring adequate replacement employment opportunities could also be made if there is an adequate degree of wage and price flexibility, that would allow rapid and smooth re-equilibration of the economy.

Finally, as mentioned in Chapter 2, it may be possible to limit the scale of the adjustment costs simply by phasing the introduction of environmental tax policy measures, and making a clear and unambiguous advance announcement of the planned profile of tax measures. Much of the economic burden of adjustment arises when a large amount of adjustment is required in a short period of time, straining the natural capacity of the economy to absorb change and create new employment opportunities. The more gradual the pace of change in policy, the more likely it will be that environmental tax policies can be implemented without major transitional costs falling on any segment of the population.

4.5. Conclusions

There is a very limited empirical literature on the distributional effects of environmental taxes and possible compensating measures. Nonetheless, a number of conclusions can be drawn from the available literature about the main distributional issues, and the scope for them to be addressed through compensating policy adjustments.

Distributional issues matter for policy, both for "objective" and "pragmatic" reasons. In the first case, there may be policy objectives concerning the position of particular groups, such as the poor or the elderly, which concern policy-makers. In the second case, if the gains and losses from environmental tax policies are too unevenly distributed, the losers may form a powerful lobby opposing the introduction of environmental taxes.

The distributional issues that arise with environmental taxes are greater than with economic instruments which do not raise revenues. Although all environmental policies may involve distributional gainers and losers – the pattern of abatement costs may be unevenly distributed, for example, or the environmental benefits may not accrue evenly to all groups in society – environmental taxes raise, in addition, the possibility that the burden of tax payments may be unevenly distributed. In most cases, this is probably the most significant distributional issue. There is less evidence that other effects are very unevenly distributed, or that they are more unevenly distributed if environmental taxes are used than if other policy instruments are employed.

The principal environmental taxes raising distributional issues of any practical significance are environmental taxes on energy, especially those which would impose substantial additional taxation on domestic energy. In some OECD countries, domestic energy has the character of a necessity in household budgets, and taxes on domestic energy are correspondingly regressive.

There is a range of possible ways in which policy could offset undesired distributional effects of environmental taxes. Mitigation measures may in fact undermine the environmental effectiveness of the tax. Compensation measures would be more appropriate, but each option carries its limitations based on each country's taxation and social systems. An equal lump sum amount returned to each household corresponding to the average household ecotax payment would be more than sufficient to offset the regressivity of the ecotax.

It may be difficult to adequately compensate poorer households for the regressive burden of environmental taxes on energy by adjustments to the tax system alone. Poor households pay relatively little taxes, and using the tax system to return revenues to poor households will generally return much larger amounts of revenue to better-off households. Reduction in sales tax would be more successful at reducing the regressivity of environmental taxes than income tax. Recall also that compensation would already take place through the current public transfer systems. Special adjustments to social security payments and unemployment insurance payments could have adverse effects and reduce the incentive to work. A more targeted approach to compensation, perhaps including reduced energy costs for the vulnerable poor, particularly the elderly, or measures to improve the energy efficiency of their homes, may be required.

Where households are prevented by market failures from adjusting efficiently to higher energy prices, their reductions in energy consumption in response to higher energy prices will tend to be smaller, and more "painful" in terms of their welfare cost. The social and distributional costs of higher energy prices may be exacerbated if market failures in energy efficiency investment are particularly concentrated amongst low income households, or other vulnerable groups. Measures to rectify the underlying market failures would then have the twin merits that they would tend to reduce the aggregate economic cost of achieving a given reduction in consumption, and at the same time would also help to reduce the social and distributional cost of higher energy taxation.

Notes

1. Households classified by age of head of household.
2. In practice, the level of carbon tax needed would presumably be less than this, because of substitutions between fuels, and between energy and other inputs to production.

References

BAKER, P., McKAY, S. and SYMONS, E. (1990), ''The Simulation of Indirect Tax Reforms: the IFS Simulation Program for Indirect Taxation (SPIT)'', IFS Working Paper No. 90/11, London Institute for Fiscal Studies.

BALLARD, SHOVEN and WHALLEY, (1985), ''General Equilibrium Computations of the Marginal Welfare Costs of Taxes in the United States'', American Economic Review, Vol. 75, pp. 128-138.

BARKER, T. and JOHNSTONE, N. (1993), ''The Interdependence of Equity and Efficiency Objectives in Fiscal Policies to Reduce Carbon Emissions in the Domestic Sector'', University of Cambridge, Department of Applied Economics, Energy-Environment-Economy Modelling Discussion Paper No. 6.

BLUNDELL, R., PASHARDES, P. and WEBER, G. (1989), ''What do we Learn about Consumer Demand Patterns from Microdata?'', Institute for Fiscal Studies and London Business School, Micro to Macro Papers No. 3, London.

BOHM, P. (1991), ''Taxation and Environment: The Case of Sweden'', in OECD.

BRECHLING, V., HELM, D. and SMITH, S. (1991), ''Domestic Energy Conservation: Environmental Objectives and Market Failures'', in D. Helm (ed.), Economic Policy towards the Environment, Oxford Basil Blackwell Ltd.

BRECHLING, V. and SMITH, S. (1994), ''Household Energy Efficiency in the UK'', Fiscal Studies, Vol. 15, No. 2, pp. 44-56.

BURTRAW, D. and PORTNEY, P.R. (1991), The Role of Compensation in Implementing Market-Based Environmental Policies, Resources for the Future, Washington, DC.

CASLER, S. D. and RAFIQUI, A. (1993), ''Evaluating Fuel Tax Equity: Direct and Indirect Distributional Effects'', National Tax Journal, Vol. 46, pp. 197-205.

COMMON, M. S. (1985), ''The Distributional Implications of Higher Energy Prices in the UK'', Applied Economics, Vol. 17, pp. 421-436.

Congressional Budget Office (1990), Federal Taxation of Tobacco, Alcoholic Beverages, and Motor Fuels, Congress of the United States, Congressional Budget Office, Washington, DC.

CRAWFORD, I., SMITH, S. and WEBB, S. (1993), VAT on Domestic Energy, IFS Commentary London Institute for Fiscal Studies.

HARRISON, D. and PORTNEY, P. R. (1982), ''Who Loses from Reform of Environmental Regulation'' in W.A. Magat (ed.) Reform of Environmental Regulation, Ballinger Publishing Company, Cambridge, MA.

JOHNSON, P., McKAY, S. and SMITH, S. (1990) The Distributional Consequences of Environmental Taxes, IFS Commentary No. 23, London The Institute for Fiscal Studies.

MADDOCK, R. and CASTAÑO, E. (1991), ''The Welfare Impact of Rising Block Pricing: Electricity in Colombia'', The Energy Journal, Vol. 12, No. 9, pp. 65-77.

Ministry of Economic Affairs, Denmark (1993), ''Lovmodel''. Overview of the Danish Law Model System. Copenhagen Ministry of Economic Affairs.

OECD (1992), Climate Change: Designing a Practical Tax System, OECD, Paris.

OECD (1993), Environmental Policies and Industrial Competitiveness, OECD, Paris.

OECD (1994), The Distributive Effects of Economic Instruments for Environmental Policy, OECD, Paris.

OECD (1995) Climate Change, Economic Instruments and Income Distribution, OECD, Paris, 1995.

PEARSON, M. and SMITH, S. (1991), ''The European Carbon Tax: An Assessment of the European Commission's Proposals'', London The Institute for Fiscal Studies.

PITTEVILS, I. (1995), ''A European Carbon/Energy Tax? Taking Care of Environment and Competitiveness. A Difficult Task'', Documentatieblad Ministerie van Financien, Belgium, January-February 1995, pp. 81-126.

POTERBA, J. M. (1991), ''Designing a Carbon Tax'', in R. Dornbusch and J. M. Poterba (eds.), Global Warming: Economic Policy Responses, Cambridge Massachusetts, The MIT Press.

POTERBA, J.M. (1989), ''Lifetime Incidence and the Distributional Burden of Excise Taxes'', American Economic Review, Papers and Proceedings, Vol. 79, pp. 325-30.

RAJAH, N. and SMITH, S. (1993), ''Distributional Aspects of Household Water Charges'', Fiscal Studies, Vol. 14, No. 3, pp. 86-108.

SCHILLO, B., GIANARELLI, L., KELLY, D., SWANSON, S. and WILCOXEN, P. (1992), The Distributional Impacts of a Carbon Tax, mimeo, Energy Policy Branch, US EPA.

SCOTT, S. (1992), Theoretical Considerations and Estimates of the Effects on Households, in J. FitzGerald and D. McCoy (eds.), The Economic Effects of Carbon Taxes, pp. 11-34, Policy Research Series, Paper No. 14, The Economic and Social Research Institute, Dublin.

SMITH, S. (1992), "The Distributional Consequences of Taxes on Energy and the Carbon Content of Fuels", European Economy, Special Issue No. 1/1992. "The economics of limiting CO_2 emissions", pp. 241-268.

SMITH, S. (1994), "Who Pays for Climate Change Policies? Distributional Side-Effects and Policy Responses", in OECD (1994), The Economics of Climate Change: Proceedings of an OECD/IEA Conference, OECD, Paris, pp. 277-291.

SYMONS, E., PROOPS, J. and P. GAY (1994), "Carbon Taxes, Consumer Demand and Carbon Dioxide Emissions: a Simulation Analysis for the UK", Fiscal Studies, Vol. 15, No. 2, pp. 19-43.

Chapter 5

THE USE OF REVENUES FROM ENVIRONMENTAL TAXES

Among the class of environmental taxes, only taxation of fossil fuels (a carbon or energy tax) is likely to raise significant amounts of revenue; these taxes, hereafter simply described as energy taxes, are therefore the focus of this chapter. Many of the issues raised, such as the possible pre-emption of receipts to pay for compensation to those losing from the new tax, are relevant to user charges and environmental levies which raise small amounts of revenue. But these will not have the macro-economic impact of the major structural shift in taxation implied by an energy tax.

5.1. Alternative uses of revenues

Interest in the use of the revenues is motivated by two main issues. First, any beneficial economic effects from disbursing the revenues may reduce the gross economic cost of securing an improved environment. Many empirical studies have not paid sufficient attention to the way energy tax receipts are spent. Secondly, the revenues may be used in ways to generate political acceptance of the new tax, among both the consumers and producers who are affected by the new tax and among the electorate in general. Both of these issues have been referred to in earlier chapters.

There are at least three main options for using the revenues from an environmental tax open to governments: increasing expenditure on particular public programmes, reducing budget deficits and reducing other taxes. The most appropriate use will vary with the particular circumstances of the country concerned: the size of the budget deficit and of the current tax burden, the functioning of capital and labour markets, consumption patterns, the design of the tax system and the country's natural endowments. These factors will together determine which other taxes are the most distortionary, and also which potential reform will have the greatest source of efficiency gains, and the implications of an energy tax for a country's competitiveness.

One potential use for revenues is to respond to pressure to compensate those most affected by the energy tax, as discussed in detail in Chapter 4, particularly if the tax is regressive. This pressure may result in revenues raised being pre-empted for expenditure on transfer payments or for compensatory reductions in other taxes to offset the impact on consumers who are disproportionately affected by the new tax. Producer interests may also push for compensating measures, especially for regional or sectoral assistance for workers and firms in energy intensive areas (see Chapter 3). As in the case of Switzerland, the government may also decide to return the revenues directly to the taxpayers. In any case, the design of a compensation scheme should always ensure that it avoids weakening or eliminating the incentive effect of the tax.

A second option on the public expenditure side of the accounts is to "earmark" the revenues for environmental expenditure. This might promote political acceptability of the tax by portraying the measure as an environmental rather than simply a revenue raising exercise. Hypothecating these marginal revenues would only make any economic sense if the revenues fund genuinely additional environmental projects and the level and allocation of other expenditure is irrevocably set. If government (implicitly or otherwise) simply offsets the additional environmental expenditure earmarked from the tax by cutting generally funded spending, then the hypothecation would merely be a political exercise to generate acceptance of the new tax. The main argument against earmarking is that it could prevent governments from optimising the composition of government spending. This and other issues related to earmarking are presented in Chapter 2.

Financing a reduction in the public sector deficit may be a priority for energy taxes in countries with a particularly large deficit or public sector debt level. Assuming that a rate of growth of government debt that exceeds the interest rate cannot be sustained in the long term, such a strategy may be viewed as equivalent to a reduction in the future tax burden.

There are a number of potential choices for using environmental tax receipts to reduce other taxes. The attractiveness of this option as opposed to increased public spending or deficit reduction may depend on the current aggregate tax burden and tax structure in the country concerned.

The distortionary cost of a carbon or energy tax depends on the existing level of subsidy to or taxation of energy. Adding a new tax to an already high level of tax will more than proportionately increase the economic cost compared with a situation where a particular energy source is not taxed. One option, therefore, for the use of new environmental tax revenues is to reduce existing energy taxes where these are already high, for example, petrol excises (see for instance, the Swedish tax reform).

The revenues may also be used to reduce more general consumption taxes. While this is likely to be a political priority in only a few countries, it has the economic benefit of reducing the inflationary impact of the new tax.

Using environmental tax revenues to reduce taxes on labour has been widely proposed, as a way of delivering a so-called "double dividend"[1] of both a cleaner environment and increased employment (see Section 5.3 below).[2] Others have termed the link between environmental and employment policy a "spurious coalition" (Mors, 1994), arguing that environmental taxes should be introduced primarily for environmental reasons – if they are a means of achieving maximum environmental benefits with the lowest overall abatement costs compared with other policy measures – and not as part of employment policy. Indeed, the theory of economic policy-making argues that the number of instruments employed should not be fewer than the number of policy objectives. However, environmental taxes may have a "spill-over" effect into other policy areas, such as energy policy and taxation. Workers in energy-intensive industries may see a fall in the demand for their services. If they have firm- or even industry-specific human capital, they may be unable to move into other industries. In countries with rigid real wages and other labour market inflexibilities, environmental taxes will reduce employment. The extent of the fall in employment depends on how much of the tax burden falls on labour.

5.2. The incidence of an environmental tax

The fundamental question is which economic agents bear the costs of the energy tax, not in the sense of the process of paying the tax but in the economic sense of facing a loss of welfare. This is a complex question in this case as with most taxes. A number of agents are affected: resource owners, workers, owners of capital and consumers. With the imposition of the tax, a fall in demand will reduce the value of resources, owners of capital may find the rate of return on their investment falling, and a lower level of demand for labour may result in higher unemployment or lower real wages. These losses may affect domestic or foreign producers (*i.e.* not resident in the country imposing the tax), or both. Any increase in prices resulting from the tax will reduce the purchasing power of consumers' incomes, although many consumers, of course, are also workers consuming out of labour income, or owners of capital and financing consumption from the investment return. The other major group of consumers of interest are those whose primary income source is transfer payments (see also Chapter 4).

The precise allocation of the burden of the energy tax between these groups depends on a number of economic variables, the design of the tax, and whether short- or long-term effects are being considered. Figure 5.1 provides a simplified guide to the discussion of these mechanisms. It is inevitably a simplification, and the branches do not represent mutually exclusive potential outcomes.

5.3. Taxes on energy resource owners

If a country or group of countries introducing an energy tax has a sufficiently large impact on worldwide demand, resource owners may bear the brunt of the tax. For example, a fossil fuel tax introduced by a number of OECD Member countries would reduce the oil price, improving the terms of trade of oil-importing countries at the expense of the oil-producing countries. In contrast, an oil exporting country could shift the burden of its environmental policies onto foreign consumers, by restricting supply and so raising its world market price. Since much of the energy used in OECD countries comes from domestically owned resources, the tax burden cannot be shifted entirely onto foreign resource owners.

Public ownership of energy resources is also common among OECD countries. In these cases, public sector revenues would be reduced if the tax burden could not be passed on to consumers as a result of fewer profits or greater losses earned by nationalised industries. Where public ownership is not the norm, energy producers and utilities tend to be subject to public sector regulation. Under rate of return regulation, the tax could result in a more than proportionate increase in prices, with little of the tax falling on resource owners. The impact is less clear cut in a price regulation regime, depending on the response of the regulator concerned, although if price regulations are not changed (at least in the short-term) then resource owners will again bear the tax, although some of this may be shifted onto labour in the affected sectors.

If resource owners are able to pass on the tax burden, who bears the final incidence depends on the structure of the energy tax, in particular, whether it is levied purely on final consumption or earlier in the production and distribution process, thereby affecting production costs.

A consumption based energy tax

An energy tax levied only on final consumption – as opposed to one levied earlier in the production and distribution chain – has no direct effect on the structure of costs of production. The analysis of such a tax is therefore broadly similar to that of any consumption tax. In fact, most actual and proposed taxes would be a combination of effects on production and consumption, but it is useful to discuss these impacts separately.

Figure 5.1. Incidence of an energy tax

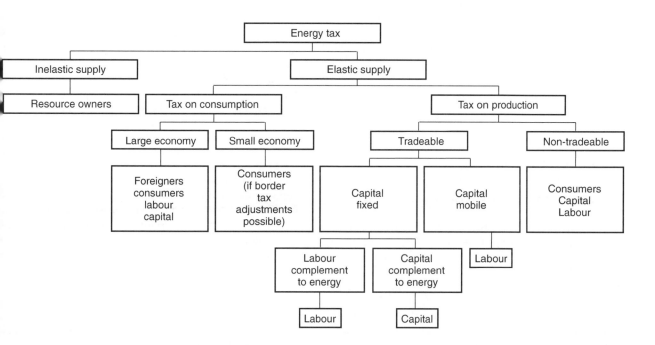

Source: OECD.

The incidence of a consumption based energy tax depends on the impact of the tax on the pattern of world-wide demand. If the country or group of countries introducing the tax is sufficiently large to affect relative prices, then part of the tax burden will be transferred to producers (labour and capital) in energy intensive industry both domestically and abroad. If the country is small, world relative prices are unaffected. If border tax adjustments are possible (levying the appropriate tax on the energy used in production of imports), then consumers will bear the tax burden. If these adjustments are not possible (either for reasons of administrative complexity or as a result of international trade obligations, see Chapter 3), then purely domestic producers will lose, as consumers are able to buy imports at the tax-exclusive price.

A production based energy tax

Determining the incidence of a production based tax is more complex. Consumers will again bear part of the tax, depending on the influence of the country or group of countries introducing the tax on worldwide demand and prices and on the possibility of operating border tax adjustments. The remaining part will be borne by capital

or labour, depending on the production structure and the factor supply elasticities and on whether the output of a particular sector is traded internationally or not.

A major determinant of supply elasticities is the degree to which factors are able to move abroad to escape the tax. Capital and energy are relatively more mobile internationally, particularly in the long-term, and if only a few countries introduce the energy tax, opportunities for moving to avoid it are enhanced. In these circumstances, the tax will fall on non-mobile labour. In the short-term, however, physical capital is also likely to be immobile. Which of the two fixed factors (labour or capital) is most affected depends on their relative substitutability for energy. Empirical evidence suggests that energy and capital are complements, so, at least in the short-term, capital bears some of the burden of the energy tax (Bovenberg and van der Ploeg, 1994). But shifting the tax burden from capital to labour has a cost. If investment fell as a result of the lower post-tax return, then labour productivity will be reduced. Wages will adjust to reflect the decline in productivity and so the tax burden will shift back to labour. If, by contrast, the industry in question produces non-tradeable output, the greater part of the tax will be borne by domestic consumers.

67

Tax exemptions for energy intensive sectors

One way of protecting workers most affected by an energy tax is to exempt energy intensive sectors. Many existing and proposed environmental taxes include such exemptions, which are sometimes limited to sectors open to international competition or subject to certain abatement targets being met (see Chapter 2 and Annex). Such exemptions can be distortionary and they encourage rent-seeking behaviour across the dividing line between sectors. Relative prices may be shifted to the disadvantage of labour intensive sectors. Furthermore, by reducing the environmental effectiveness of the tax, they undermine the case for introducing it.

The sustainability of energy tax revenues

There is a trade-off between the environmental and the revenue-raising objectives of an energy tax. If the demand for energy is relatively inelastic, the revenues raised will be relatively large, but as demand for energy is little changed the environmental impact will be smaller. Elastic energy demand would have the opposite effect: the reduction in energy use and the resulting environmental benefits would be relatively large but the revenue generated would be smaller. This effect will vary over the time horizon considered. Although energy demand may be relatively inelastic in the short-run due to adjustment costs, in the long-run consumers and producers may shift to a more energy (or carbon) efficient capital stock. The revenues from an energy tax may not therefore prove fully sustainable in the long-term.

The mechanism whereby a shift to a more energy-efficient capital stock may diminish the revenue has implications for the issue of international capital mobility. If firms are able to improve energy efficiency through innovation and replacement of the capital stock, there is less incentive to move abroad to avoid the energy tax. Conversely, if capital is immobile, the incentive to adopt improved production methods will be enhanced.

The impact on employment

The effect of energy taxes on employment depends on the design of the tax, on substitution elasticities between factors of production, on whether output is traded and on the degree of international co-ordination in the introduction of the tax. A production-based tax encourages substitution of labour for energy, both at firm level and in the macroeconomy as the industrial structure shifts from energy intensive to labour intensive sectors, but the overall employment effect also depends on the supply responses of other factors. If labour is fixed and other factors are mobile, much of the incidence of the tax will fall on labour. Energy taxes on consumption have a lesser effect on employment than production-based taxes in sectors where output is traded and factors other than labour are mobile.

5.4. Environmental taxes and complementary policies

An improved environment requires adjustment to the structure of economies, with a contraction of polluting sectors and an expansion of other industries. A well-functioning market mechanism is necessary to ensure that this adjustment process proceeds smoothly. Flexible relative wages ensure that workers are given the correct signals, and the tax and benefit systems should contain incentives to encourage the re-allocation of labour to less-polluting sectors. The OECD Jobs Study (OECD, 1994a) made a series of recommendations to countries to increase flexibility in wage-setting, pursue active rather than passive labour market measures, improve skills and competences and reform unemployment benefit systems. In some countries the most appropriate response to the negative employment consequences of an energy tax may be institutional reform and investment in active labour market programmes, perhaps financed by the revenues from the energy tax.

The OECD Jobs Study also recommended that countries should "reduce direct taxes on those with low earnings" and "ensure that low-paid workers are better off in work compared with relying entirely on social benefits by providing ... low average tax rates on low-wage workers relative to benefit incomes, or in-work supplements to low paid workers".[3] Unemployment tends to be concentrated on low-skilled labour, with low potential earnings.

There have been many proposals that the revenues from an energy tax should be used to reduce tax rates on labour. The overall effect of a such a shift in taxes is an empirical question, dependent on the extent to which labour bears the environmental tax burden (as discussed above), on the burden of labour taxation and on the sensitivity of employment to taxes on labour.

Taxes on labour

Figure 5.2 shows marginal effective tax rates on labour imposed on the earnings of the average production worker in a selection of OECD Member countries. The figure shows the size of the tax "wedge" on labour i.e. the difference between the cost to the employer of an additional, marginal increase in earnings and the amount received by the employee. It includes the effects of social security contributions and personal income taxes, but consumption taxes (such as excises and VAT) and other labour costs (e.g. pension contributions) are ignored. It differs from the conventional calculation of marginal tax rates, since employers' social security contributions are included in both the numerator and the denominator; it can therefore be thought of as the marginal tax rate on employers' gross labour costs. The calculation is carried out at the earnings of the average production worker in each country. Care is required in generalising the results since the tax wedge varies with income due to the rate

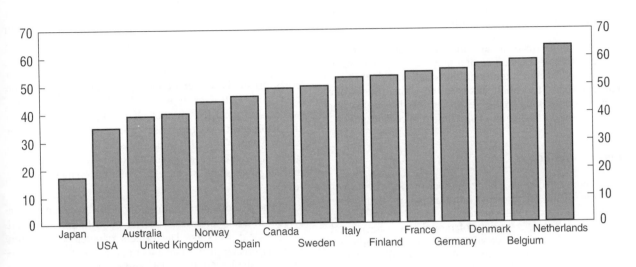

Figure 5.2. Marginal tax rate on gross labour costs, single person at earnings of average production worker in selected OECD countries, 1992

Note : The marginal tax rate on gross labour costs including social security contributions and personal income taxes. Non-wage labour costs other than social security contributions are excluded, such as contributions for private sector social provision. The personal income taxes take no account of "non-standard" reliefs, such as those for mortgage payments (see OECD, 1994c for a detailed discussion of these limitations). The effect of consumption taxes on the purchasing power of the net wage is excluded (see OECD, 1994b and 1995 which examine the effect of consumption taxes). The calculation is carried out at the earnings of the average production worker in each country (see OECD, 1994c fo a discussion of the validity of this choice of earnings level).
Source : OECD (1995).

structure of income tax and social security contributions, although OECD (1995) shows that the relative tax wedge between countries is well correlated across a large income range.

The tax wedge exceeds 60 per cent in the Netherlands – which means that the employee receives barely a third of the cost to the employer of any marginal increase in earnings – and is greater than one half in seven of the 15 countries shown. Tax wedges increased in many OECD countries during the 1980s. The desirability of cuts in labour taxes will vary with the tax burden, which, as the figure shows, differs significantly among countries.

Labour taxation, real wages and employment

Tax cuts need not necessarily reduce unemployment if wages are flexible, and so adjust to equalise supply and demand. But if labour market institutions, minimum wages or effective floors to wages generated by benefits systems prevent wages falling sufficiently to adjust for the tax wedge, unemployment will result. Any tax which reduces net income or reduces available consumption out of labour income (such as consumption taxes) encourages labour to press for wage increases to protect real take home pay. The labour market effect of taxation is likely to vary among countries, depending on the institu-

tional structure of pay bargaining and on the degree of competition in product markets, which encourages employers to resist increases in real wages in response to tax rises. Empirical evidence shows that the responsiveness of employment to labour taxes varies among countries. In Canada and Germany real wages are highly resistant to tax changes, while in Sweden, the United Kingdom and the United States, increases in taxes are mainly reflected in lower wages. Other countries – Australia, Finland, France, Italy and Japan – lie between these extremes.[4]

Taxes on capital

In countries where wages are highly flexible, cutting labour taxes will deliver only small employment benefits. In these economies, capital taxation may be more distortionary than labour taxes, suggesting that easing the tax burden here may have greater economic benefits, including effects on employment. Increased investment in response to a lower tax level raises labour productivity and so increases employment. Ballard, Shoven and Whalley (1985) use a general equilibrium framework to compute the marginal excess burden – the reduction in welfare from a small increase in a particular tax as a proportion of the tax increase – for different taxes in the United States. They found an excess burden of taxation of 33 per cent of revenues raised, varying between 23 per cent for payroll taxes, 31 per cent for income taxes and 46 per cent for capital taxes. Goulder (1994) concludes "most empirical studies of the United States indicate that capital taxes have higher marginal excess burdens than do labour taxes". Thus, in some countries capital taxes may be more distortionary than taxes on labour, and hence reducing taxes on capital may be a priority use for energy tax revenues, although the small marginal excess burdens found for labour taxes in the United States may partly be explained by the relatively low labour tax burden and the high degree of flexibility in real wages.

Empirical evidence

There have been a large number of empirical investigations of the effect of the introduction of energy taxes of different types, with the revenues used to cut a range of different taxes. A variety of models have been used: neo-classical comparative static, general equilibrium and macroeconometric. An example of the first type is Bovenberg and de Mooij (1994). OECD (1992) and Manne and Richels (1992) are examples of general equilibrium models and European Commission (1994), DRI (1993) and Standaert (1992) use macroeconomic models to investigate the economic impact of energy taxes. Within these broad classes, models differ in their treatment of factor mobility, wage determination and labour supply behaviour.

A survey of these models and their results is beyond the scope of this report. The results of the European Commission's (1994) investigation using the Quest macroeconomic model are representative of studies on European economies. The European Commission study examines the impact of a carbon/energy tax of US$ 10 per barrel of oil, amounting to 1.1 per cent of GDP or 2 to 3 per cent of government revenues. This is used to finance a cut in employers' social security contributions. The results show an increase of GDP of 0.4 per cent in the short-term, rising to 1 per cent in the medium-term (after seven years). Unemployment is predicted to fall by 0.3 per cent in the first year, and 0.9 per cent in the medium-term.

A number of other studies on energy taxes in European economies have found similar effects. For example, Standaert (1992) using the Hermes macroeconomic model for France, Germany, Italy and the United Kingdom found a 0.5 per cent increase in employment (although a 0.1 per cent reduction in GDP) in the medium-term. The Planning Bureau (1993), Bréchet (1992) and FitzGerald and McCoy (1992) find medium-term GDP increases of between zero and 0.5 per cent and employment growth of between 0.4 and 0.7 per cent in macroeconomic models of Belgium, France and Ireland respectively.

Similar exercises have been carried out in the United States, although the main focus of the results has been on output rather than employment effects. Shackleton (1992) surveys results from four models, where the revenues are used to cut personal income taxes, payroll taxes and corporate income taxes. Again, a mix of different models was used, including both macroeconometric – DRI and Wharton Econometrics-LINK – and general equilibrium – Goulder (1994) and Jorgensen and Wilcoxen. In the medium-term, both macro models predict higher GDP growth if the revenues are used to cut employer payroll taxes, although short-term predictions differ. In the DRI model, lower labour costs offset the effect of the energy tax on production costs and GDP rises above the baseline after two years, whereas in the LINK model GDP drops significantly in the short-term and only rises above the baseline after seven years. This difference arises from assumptions about the incidence of payroll taxes between employers and employees, and so the effect of a tax change on wage levels.

The European Commission also investigated the effects of a cut in social security contributions targeted on low-paid workers. The effects of such a reduction were far greater than the results of an across the board cut reported above: GDP in the medium-term was 1.8 per cent higher compared with 1 per cent under a general reduction, and unemployment down 2.7 per cent compared with 0.9 per cent. The results of this extension of the analysis depend critically on the degree of substitution of low-skilled for high-skilled labour as their relative prices change due to the tax shift.[5] This factor explains the difference in results between the targeted and the general tax reduction.

These modelling exercises assume that all the revenues raised by the energy tax are available for cutting other taxes, and not, for example, used to compensate those reliant on transfer payments. Increases in transfers to those in the labour force or on the margins of the labour force offset one of the key feedback mechanisms for increasing employment: the reduction in the replacement rate (the ratio of net income in work to net income out of work) that results from the cut in labour taxes. Increased transfers to those outside the labour force will have fewer economic benefits than reductions in labour taxes when these are distortionary.

Reducing the most distortionary taxes in an economy (be they labour, capital or consumption taxes) is the most appropriate policy to follow if the revenues are not used for public expenditure or reducing budget deficits. However, modelling exercises which look at the economic effects of using energy taxes to reduce the most distortionary tax are over-stating the benefits of the tax shift. Employment-increasing tax reforms are open to governments substituting other less distortionary taxes for the least efficient tax. In this case, the introduction of the environmental tax is not a necessary condition for achieving efficiency gains, and so the measurement of economic benefits in many modelling exercises conflates the improvement attributable to the environmental tax with benefits attainable in its absence. The European Commission Quest model was also used to investigate a switch from social security contributions to personal income taxes of the same order of magnitude as the energy tax; the effect on unemployment was a 0.7 per cent reduction in the income tax case, compared with 0.9 per cent in the energy tax case. Empirical measures of the benefits of a switch to an energy tax should be measured against a tax of representative inefficiency, and not against the most distortionary.

This argument also applies to the comparison of targeted and general tax reductions. The difference between the two sets of results is driven by the restructuring of social security contributions to reduce the relative burden on the low paid. The energy tax is not necessary for these efficiency gains to be reaped.

All empirical models necessarily involve simplifications, and it is not possible to model all the feedback mechanisms illustrated in Figure 5.1. In particular, none of the macro or general equilibrium models is able to address adequately the issue of international mobility of capital. While this may not be important in the short-term, in the medium-term the effect may be significant.

There are many grounds for interpreting the results of these studies and the policy messages they contain with caution. For these reasons, the OECD Jobs Study [OECD (1994a)] concluded that "there is increasing agreement, at least in countries where the taxes are high, that part of the base for social security financing should be shifted away from taxes that add directly to labour costs. Evidence suggests that a significant revenue-neutral cut in social security contributions could increase employment over the medium term in those countries where wages and prices are sticky. But it would be unrealistic to expect large long-run declines in unemployment in response to tax shifting. Contributions could, however, be cut in a way that favours the hiring of low-wage, unskilled labour by eliminating the ceilings on employer contribution rates and by reducing the income tax burden on low-skilled workers."

5.5. Conclusions

The desirability of different uses of energy tax revenues will vary with the circumstances of the country introducing the tax. Like any other tax, an energy tax will face political resistance and economic resistance, in the form of pressure for compensation in the form of higher transfer payments, higher wages and industrial assistance. The revenues from the energy tax provide an opportunity for offsetting the cost of pollution abatement, but do not themselves provide a rationale for introducing a new tax: the argument rests primarily on the environmental benefits.

The allocation of energy tax revenues to deficit reduction, increased government spending or reduced taxes will simply be a reflection of the general debate about the public finances. Depending on a country's fiscal position, deficit reduction may be the most appropriate use of the ecotax revenues; in other countries, tax cuts may be a priority. There is no *a priori* correct use of the revenues, although if it is considered that other taxes should be reduced to avoid an increase in the aggregate tax burden, then it would be most appropriate to reduce more distortionary taxes.

Notes

1. The term "double dividend" is used in different ways in different studies: either welfare, GDP or employment improvements in conjunction with environmental benefits.
2. See OECD (1993), Pearce (1991), Oates (1991) and Repetto *et al.* (1992).
3. OECD (1994a), pp. 46 and 49 respectively.
4. Tyrväinen (1994). A summary of studies of the link between taxation and real wages is provided on p. 247 of OECD (1994b) and in Chapter 4 of OECD (1995).
5. The European Commission assumed an elasticity of 1.5. This is sufficiently large to generate sizeable employment shifts, although at the low end of what few empirical estimates are available (Freeman, 1986 and Hamermesh, 1985).

References

BALLARD, C.L., SHOVEN, J.B. and WHALLEY, J. (1985), "General Equilibrium Computations of the Marginal Welfare Costs of Taxes in the United States", *American Economic Review*, Vol. 75, No. 1, pp. 128-138.

BOVENBERG, A.L. and van der PLOEG, F. (1994), "Consequences of Environmental Tax Reform for Involuntary Unemployment and Welfare", Center discussion paper No. 9408, Tilburg University.

BOVENBERG, A.L. and de MOOIJ, R. (1994), "Environmental Policy in a Small Open Economy with Distortionary Labour Taxes: a General Equilibrium Analysis", Centre for Economic Policy Research (OFCEB), Erasmus University, Rotterdam, research paper No. 9304, and forthcoming, *European Journal of Political Economy*.

BRÉCHET, T. (1992), *Energy Tax in Europe: A VAT Variant with Hermes-Link*, Erasme, Paris.

DRI (1993), *The Economic Consequences of the Proposed Energy/Carbon Tax*, Brussels.

EUROPEAN COMMISSION (1994), "Taxation, Employment and Environment: Fiscal Reform for Reducing Unemployment", *European Economy*, No. 56, pp. 137-177.

FREEMAN, R.B. (1986), "Demand for Education", pp. 357-386 in Ashenfelter, O.C. and Layard, P.R.G. (eds.), *Handbook of Labour Economics*, North Holland, Amsterdam.

GOULDER, L.H. (1994), "Effects of Carbon Taxes in an Economy with Prior Tax Distortions: an Intertemporal General Equilibrium Analysis", mimeo., Stanford University and National Bureau of Economic Research.

HAMERMESH, D.P. (1985), "Substitution between Different Categories of Labour, Relative Wages and Youth Unemployment", *OECD Economic Studies*, No. 5, pp. 57-68.

MANNE, A.S. and RICHELS, R.G. (1992), *The EC Proposal for Combining Carbon and Energy Taxes*, EPRI.

MORS, M. (1994), "Employment, Revenues and Resource Taxes: Genuine Link or Spurious Coalition?", paper presented at *Emerging Policies for European Energy*, London, November.

OATES, W.E. (1991), "Pollution Charges as a Source of Public Revenues", Resources for the Future, discussion paper No. QE92-05, Washington, DC.

OECD (1992), "The Economic Cost of Reducing CO_2 Emissions", *OECD Economic Studies*, No. 19.

OECD (1993), *Taxation and the Environment: Complementary Policies*, OECD, Paris.

OECD (1994a), *The OECD Jobs Study: Facts, Analysis, Strategies*, OECD, Paris.

OECD (1994b), *The OECD Jobs Study: Evidence and Explanations*, OECD, Paris.

OECD (1994c), *The Tax/Benefit Position of Production Workers, Annual Report 1990-93*, OECD, Paris.

OECD (1995), *The OECD Jobs Study: Taxation, Employment and Unemployment*, OECD, Paris.

PEARCE, D.W. (1991), "The Role of Carbon Taxes in Adjusting to Global Warming", *Economic Journal*, Vol. 101, pp. 938-948.

REPETTO, R., DOWER, R.C., JENKINS, R. and GEOGHEGAN, J. (1992), "Green Fees: How a Tax Shift can Work for the Environment and the Economy", World Resources Institute, Washington, DC.

SHACKLETON, R. (1992), *The Efficiency Value of Carbon Tax Revenues*, United States Environmental Protection Agency, Washington, DC.

STANDAERT, S. (1992), "The Macro-Sectoral Effects of an EC-Wide Energy Tax: Simulation Experiments for 1992-2005", *European Economy*, special edition No. 1, pp. 127-151.

TYRVÄINEN, T. (1994), "Real Wage Resistance and Unemployment: Multivariate Analysis of Co-Integrating Relations in 10 OECD Economies", *OECD Jobs Study Working Paper* series.

Chapter 6

SUMMARY AND CONCLUSIONS

6.1. A new trend in environmental policy

Recent OECD work has identified major advantages to a greater use of market mechanisms in environmental policy, compared to a "command and control" approach based on environmental regulations and concluded that "environment and fiscal policies can and should be made mutually reinforcing".* Environmental taxes serve to change relative prices and help ensure that producers and consumers take account of the effects of their activities on the environment. As opposed to command and control measures, ecotaxes can provide greater flexibility to polluters who are free to adapt to market signals in a cost effective manner. If fixed at an appropriate level, environmental taxes minimise the overall cost of achieving a given pollution control target. They also provide a permanent incentive to reduce pollution and thus a continuing incentive to innovate in order to reduce pollution even below target levels so as to reduce tax payments. Environmental taxes may also have a certain appeal to governments since they produce revenues that would not arise with regulations. However, this does not mean that regulation no longer has a role to play in environmental policy. To the contrary, regulation and environmental taxation, and even some other economic instruments, could be undertaken as complementary measures.

There are two major approaches to environmental taxation. The first consists of a piecemeal approach where new environmental taxes are introduced to deal with newly identified environmental issues or to replace or complement existing regulations. The second approach involves a comprehensive restructuring of the tax system to achieve environmental objectives.

While there is wide consensus as to the virtues of environmental taxes, a number of implementation issues must be clearly identified and tackled. It was the mandate of the OECD Joint Sessions on Taxation and Environment to analyse these issues. Four main categories of issues have been identified and are reviewed in this report: *i*) the design and implementation of environmental taxes; *ii*) competitiveness and trade impacts; *iii*) distributive implications; and, *iv*) the use of ecotax revenues.

---

* OECD (1993), *Taxation and the Environment: Complementary Policies*, OECD, Paris.

6.2. Designing and implementing environmental taxes

While there are examples of successful implementation of environmental taxes, there are also cases where proposals have either been delayed, heavily modified or simply abandoned. Appropriate design and implementation of environmental taxes can successfully address some of the issues that have lead to these failures.

An appropriate policy framework

Environmental taxation is used to ensure that those that use environmental resources incorporate the value of their services into the prices of goods and services they provide or consume. In other words, environmental taxation is used to internalise environmental costs. Each environmental problem is different and presents various characteristics that will lead to the choice of one instrument, or a combination of taxes and regulations, and a different implementation strategy. These characteristics include market related features: the price elasticity or the availability of alternatives, the potential for technological innovation, the extent abatement costs might differ across sectors, the extent domestic sectors are in a favourable competitive position or in a fast growing market, or the market structure itself. Other characteristics include environment related features such as the seriousness of environmental damage, or whether detrimental emissions arise in a certain local area or at certain time during the year or day.

By using a comprehensive approach, policy-makers may be in a position to avoid situations whereby polluters are successful in reducing the tax base and their tax payments, but not polluting emissions. Policy makers need to understand the full production process and the environmental impacts of alternatives. They also need to review if there exists other market failures that may prevent the effective use of environmental taxes.

A clear linkage

With respect to pollution, environmental taxes forces polluters to internalise the external pollution damage costs that arise from their activities. Pollution taxes rely principally on two types of instruments: one which is directly related to emissions; and one which relies on the indirect relationship between the tax base and the pollution emitted. Generally speaking, the ''linkage'' between the tax and the environmental problem it is designed to tackle should be explicit and as close as possible to the polluting source. A direct link can easily be established when taxes are based on polluting *emissions*. Emission taxes are best when polluting emissions are emitted by stationary, easily identifiable sources. The use of emission taxes on measured levels of polluting emissions is less appropriate and may not be feasible when the polluting sources are small, varied and too numerous for individual monitoring and collection the charge. When based on the environmental characteristics of the product, *product taxes* can be particularly effective as they may offer a convenient proxy to emission taxes.

Appropriate linkage contributes to the effectiveness of the tax in several respects. A loose link would give no clear signal to economic agents as to the appropriate choice in consumption and production. A good linkage makes explicit the purpose of the tax and increases its transparency. As any new tax is likely to be controversial, the acceptability of the tax will increase if the link between the tax and the environmental problem it is designed to solve is made clear.

Ensuring acceptability

Stakeholders need to be convinced first that there is in fact an environmental problem that requires action, and second that the advocated policy will in fact contribute to its solution. A new tax has more of a chance of being accepted when people understand the rationale behind its implementation. Generally speaking, the public and taxpayers should be kept regularly informed on the objectives, operation and achievements of the tax. While the related costs of ecotaxes will easily be raised by opponents to the taxes, the authorities should also ensure that all side benefits are understood.

Consultations with stakeholders could ease implementation and provide an opportunity to both government and private sectors to acquire a more accurate knowledge of the situation. Consultations should be as wide as possible to ensure a fair representation. The availability of alternative means of consumption or production would also help increase the acceptability of an ecotax while contributing to its effectiveness. In fact, the availability of alternatives allows producers to lower their tax payments without necessarily having to lower output. In addition, targets and schedules may be helpful. The introduction of the new tax should preferably be announced in advance, and increased gradually, to allow adequate planning. Overall, the tax instrument should be predictable and relatively stable. It should be simple to understand. As much as possible it should involve relatively low administrative, monitoring and compliance costs and rely, to the extent possible, on the existing tax systems and accounting measures so as not to create excessive burden on government and industry.

The tax base: simple and explicit

There are many factors to consider when determining the appropriate tax base and the point of imposition. The essential first steps in designing the tax base is to understand clearly the life-cycle of the pollutant, that is how it is produced, used and disposed of. In fact, the tax base should differ based on the spacial quality of the environmental problem to be solved. For instance, the problem may be more acute in local areas, due to concentration of population or simply due to the geographical position of the area. Ideally, all emissions related to the pollution problem should be included in the tax base. However, the tax base should be kept relatively simple. Excessive complexity would make the tax difficult to comprehend, reduce transparency and thus affect its acceptability and implementation.

The base will also differ when pollution arises either from production and consumption. The choice between an emission and a product tax will largely depend on the monitoring possibility and cost. The number of polluters and the source of pollution, whether diffuse or point-source, will determine the point of imposition of the tax. Another important factor to consider when determining the tax base is the possibility to build on the existing tax system. Generally speaking, the availability of data on production and transactions makes product taxes easier to implement than taxes on emissions. Ideally, one should aim at minimising the number of points of collection. If imposed early in the distribution chain (*e.g.* at the point of extraction or importation), it limits the number of transactions to be monitored, and it also maximises the size of the tax base. However, if taxes are imposed early in the chain, the tax base could also include activities that are not damaging for the environment and for which a system of rebate should be set in place, increasing the administrative costs. On the other hand, in an attempt to avoid discrimination between locally produced products and imported ones, it may be necessary to locate the point of imposition closer to the retail level.

Choosing a tax rate

In theory, to fully internalise social costs, the appropriate tax rate should be set where the marginal cost of reducing emissions equals marginal social damage. This however requires a large set of information, most often not available, difficult if not impossible to acquire in time, and where estimates are based on a set of often questionable assumptions. A second-best approach consists in setting the rate according to a predetermined environmental target and the anticipated response to various changes in price signals. Because the response may end up different from what was first expected, the rate schedule may have to be adjusted. When choosing a tax rate, care should be taken to distinguish between short-term and long-term objectives. If environmental objectives are long term, the tax rate may be set initially at a much lower rate than if one seeks to achieve major results in a short period, say of one to two years. Long-term objectives allow for a more gradual approach.

The tax rate on products should be based on external costs generated by the polluting content of the product. This means that amongst substitutes, the tax differentiation should be based on the polluting content of the products to build in the right price signals. Since the pollution associated with the production or use of a particular commodity will be a function of the polluting content of the commodity rather than its value, the tax will most likely be of a specific nature rather than *ad valorem*. If the required tax is determined at a relatively high rate, it may be possible to plan the introduction of an ecotax in such a manner as to minimise possible initial negative effects, and to allow long term planning and proper investment decisions on the part of producers and consumers. However, pre-announcement may require the use of floor stocks taxes if opportunities for unintended tax evasion such as "hoarding" are to be avoided. It may also be helpful if governments announce targets and schedules in terms of environmental objectives.

Conflicts could arise between tax and environment departments if the objective of the tax is not made clear. For instance, as revenue from ecotaxes may decline over-time, environmental taxes may not be popular with tax officials as they try to plan revenues based on a determined expenditure programme. At the same time, a tax that provides a continuous flow of tax revenues may not be popular with environment officials since it could mean that the tax rate is not high enough to have any incentive effects. Short-term and long-term environmental objectives of the tax should be made clear. Officials should be aware of how the ecotax revenues fit in the whole tax base.

Adjusting for inflation

Unlike an *ad valorem* tax, the incentive effect of a specific excise tax may be eroded in times of inflation. In order to avoid this effect, the specific rate may be re-examined and if necessary readjusted periodically to reflect changes in the external costs of the pollution. Automatic indexation is not a necessity. A periodic revision of the rates may be sufficient, especially if long term environmental objectives are set. In any case, environmental taxes should be regularly reviewed to assess the extent to which they fulfil the intended purpose. Even without changes in the general price level, it may be necessary to adjust the rate because of changes in relative prices of the taxed and non-taxed substitutes (or complements).

Minimum administrative costs

It is important to assess the administrative, monitoring and compliance costs in implementing environmental taxes. The choice between an emission and a product tax will partly depend on the monitoring feasibility. A com-promise may be necessary between environmental effectiveness and the need to use cost-effective means of administering the tax. The design of the tax, such as the choice of the tax base and the point of imposition, could also affect administrative costs. Those costs and the effectiveness of the tax may also depend on which level of government and which Ministry is responsible for administering the tax and applying penalties, and monitoring environmental progress. Administrative costs will also be more important if there are rebate systems, mitigation measures or compensation programmes set in place.

Regulatory authorities: choosing the appropriate level

A major issue related to tax design and implementation strategy is the need to consider the potential tax and environment policy jurisdictions, either local, regional or national. The scope and extent of the taxing authority has an impact on the efficiency and effectiveness of any tax strategy. For instance, local authorities may be in a better position to develop the appropriate environmental policy with regard to some local pollution problem. However, as rivers or underground water often cross many jurisdictions, it may be necessary for many local authorities or some higher level jurisdiction to develop the appropriate policy. In addition, it may not be effective for local authorities to tax some products that may be easily acquired from some other jurisdictions, since the costs of enforcement may be too high.

Monitoring and evaluating

Adequate monitoring systems are needed to provide an accounting basis for levying pollution taxes and to evaluate the impacts such taxes have on overall pollution levels and on those paying the taxes. Such systems are necessary in order to calculate the amount of taxes owed and for enforcement purposes. Evaluation systems are also needed to measure the degree of success of the tax in reducing pollution and the economic impact of the tax, and to help adjust either the tax rate and/or the tax base in order to meet planned objectives. Such systems would be much easier and cheaper to operate if "built in" the tax system.

Compliance

Other design issues such as the frequency of tax payments could impose relatively large compliance costs on *small* businesses, and some adjustments may be required. For instance, some monitoring systems may not easily be affordable to small businesses.

"Tax Packaging"

As the costs of environmental taxes are often more transparent than the costs of regulations, there may be a more vocal opposition to their implementation. A number of measures may be taken to make the tax not only more efficient but also more easily acceptable. A complete "policy package" should include measures that reduces non-price barriers such as lack of information or lack of technological know-how or promotion of management tools such as environmental auditing. In some cases, government programmes that impede the effective use of environmental taxes may have to be revised. The breakdown of these barriers will increase the elasticities and will make environmental taxes more effective and more efficient.

Earmarking

Tax revenues are said to be earmarked for environmental purposes if it is decided, *in advance*, that a certain share or the totality of the revenues shall be used for some environmental programmes, even if the tax is not initially set with some environmental objectives. These programmes may be complementary to the ecotax, or could be related to some other environmental problem. If tax revenues are earmarked, the amounts granted for a specific programme will consequently vary with the tax revenues and thereby will be fixed independently of regular cost/benefit analysis and programme evaluation. This may easily lead to an inefficient allocation of resources, either because the amount of tax revenues will be too large and too much will be spent on those specific programmes, or the tax revenues will be too small and not enough resources will be devoted to the programmes. In addition, depending on the price elasticities and the possibilities of new less polluting methods of production, the revenues from the ecotax are likely to decline over time. Overall, the main argument against earmarking is that it could prevent governments from optimising the composition of government spending. In the long term, it could create inefficiencies and rigidities, and reduce the options in priority setting.

The risks of setting a precedent with earmarking should be carefully assessed. While there may currently be political demand to earmark the funds from environmental taxes, demands to earmark the funds from other taxes and charges could also arise for other social and development objectives, such as health and transport. As the share of earmarked funds rises, governments may find themselves no longer able to set priorities over time. This is true whether earmarking is used by local, regional or national governments. In any case, while resources may be necessary to help make the transition period less painful for those most affected by the tax, it does not imply that the resources have to come from the ecotax itself and not from general funding.

Despite these well-known caveats to earmarking tax revenues, many countries have opted for earmarking or related approaches in the case of environmental taxes, mainly in view of its political advantage. Earmarking is perceived as a instrument to increase the acceptability of the new tax, and help draw political support. Besides, the effectiveness of environmental policy may be enhanced in a context where environmental programmes are complementary to ecotaxes, and when the ecotax alone cannot achieve the environmental objectives. Many of the political advantages of earmarking can be secured if, instead of earmarking, governments announce at the same time an increase in expenditure on environmental programmes that are financed from general tax receipts based on proper programme evaluation of the expenditure.

The use of earmarking in the case of Economies in Transition would appear to be acceptable as a transitional measure. At present, in many Economies in Transition, environmental expenditures are largely financed by specific or general environmental funds. Such funds can be seen as effective transitional measures to catch up accumulated lags in environmental protection measures and many pollution backlogs. Environmental funds should however be seen as transitional measures. Maintaining such funds over a lasting period would eventually result in economic inefficiency. As the transition process advances, private sources and capital markets should progressively play their true role.

Earmarking is most common in local governments when there is a direct relationship between the charge and the service provided, such as for water supply and waste removal. In fact, earmarking is a necessity in the case of user charges – as taxpayers expect a service in return. It is expected and non-controversial to allocated revenues from user charges in order to cover the cost of providing a level of service to the users. The risks encountered with earmarking in general, that is overspending or lack of appropriate funding, remain with user charges as well. Such financing programmes need to be regularly reevaluated, and should not be undertaken simply by virtue of the availability of some earmarked funds.

6.3. International implications of environmental taxes

The issues of trade and competitiveness have often been at the centre of the debate when new environmental taxes were introduced or proposed, and have helped shape the policy package of current carbon/energy taxes. In many countries, firms or industry sectors were either exempted or received some form of compensation, even when the taxes were relatively small compared to the type of carbon/energy taxes proposed to help countries stabilise their carbon emissions to the 1990 level. In other proposals, some sectors were to be exempted until other countries agreed to implement similar policies.

Many factors to consider

Trade and competitiveness effects of environmental taxes need to be analysed for all types of ecotaxes. They depend on a large number of factors, and predictability of the trade effects and of the effectiveness of the environmental tax becomes extremely difficult when one takes all these factors into account. The key lesson here should be the need to recognise that the various circumstances surrounding the implementation of the tax can lead to different results.

Some important key variables could greatly influence trade flows and the effectiveness of the environmental policy. They concern mainly whether one deals with a small country that has no influence on world market prices, or a large country where impacts on terms of trade are possible; the resource endowment of the country under study in relation to the rest of the world; the mobility of factors of production; the availability of alternatives; the level of competition in the sectors; the possibilities of technological innovation; the way environmental tax revenues may be redistributed; if trade agreements would allow countries to use border tax adjustments and other trade measures to reduce the adjustments costs in their domestic economies and to ensure the effectiveness of the tax; and whether other countries implement similar policies. Overall, theoretical predictions about trade and allocation effects are not at all clear, and any models attempting to simulate trade impacts would have to be very complex. In addition, the data bases for measuring such a relationship are still scarce.

Empirical and simulation evidence

The trade impacts of environmental regulation that have been measured empirically are negligible. Some simulation studies predict strong effects only for very few sectors of the economy. In fact, most *existing* environmental taxes seem to be too low to induce discernible trade impacts. Simulation studies often concern hypothetical high carbon energy taxes, currently not in existence.

Short term versus long term behaviour

A short-term reaction of a firm to the imposition or an increase of an environmental tax could be a reduction in supply or a change in the input mix which may lead to some factors of production becoming unemployed. Some domestic firms will lower output, while those domestic firms that offer an alternative could see an increase in demand, or the gap between domestic supply and demand may be filled by foreign supplies and this would affect trade flows. For consumers, the short run adjustment would consist of a change in the consumption basket as well as a substitution through imports. These adjustment costs are by definition transitory. Over time, both producers and consumers will take actions to avoid paying an environmental tax, and this will serve to lower the effects of the policy on competitiveness. The long-run reaction of firms will typically involve either changes in the technology, or a relocation of plants, since such activities typically involve considerations with a longer time horizon. Again trade flows may be affected.

Competitiveness and short term issues

Countries compete in many different ways to attract new investments. Regulations and taxation all influence the decision to locate in one country or another. There are many other factors influencing long term profitability and the decision to locate in one country: political stability, competent labour force, easy access to raw material or to market, adequate infrastructure and transport facilities, to name just a few. In fact, while taxes in some countries may be relatively more important than in others, companies may still choose these countries because the tax revenues are used to finance infrastructure, for example, that decrease other costs to the firm. Nevertheless, some environmental taxes are bound to increase relatively more production costs, and some firms or sub-sectors may face lower profits. The competitive position of firms and industry will be most affected if there are no other easily available alternatives, or when plants are old, although in some cases, ecotaxes could simply accelerate investment in new plant. The issue of competitiveness may be less important when the economy is experiencing high growth, or when the sector itself is in a very highly innovative industry. However, a fall in the competitive position of some firms could be dramatic for the future of some regions. Short term measures may be necessary to help the industry set in place pollution abatement measures and reduce their tax payments in the medium and long term. In any case, the impact on competitiveness will depend greatly on the use of the ecotax revenues.

Environmental effectiveness and the "leakage" issue

Governments are concerned not only about the effects of an environmental tax on competitiveness but also about the effectiveness of the policy in achieving its environmental aim. This concern becomes even more important in the case of cross-border externalities. In the context of a carbon tax, leakage refers to increases in carbon emissions in non-participating regions. If a country or regions introduces a tax which reduces the comparative advantage in the taxing country, there will likely be increased production of the taxed products in the rest of world. This could lead to a substitution of domestic production for imports and at the same time to increased emissions in the rest of the world. In the case of global pollution such as carbon emissions, the environmental benefits of the tax in the taxing country could more or less become offset by increased consumption or production in other countries. This leads to the need for international cooperation.

Mitigation and compensation measures

Ecotaxes can result in different cost and distributional impacts for various firms, sectors and regions, and offsetting measures may be necessary to ensure a greater acceptance of the tax. Environmental tax revenues may be used to compensate those least able to pay new taxes. A number of possible adjustments have been proposed, such as exemptions, rebates and compensation measures for the production sectors. Compensation measures should be designed as much as possible in a way that does not eliminate or reduce the economic incentives of the tax, or reduce its economic efficiency and environmental effectiveness.

Compensation schemes could clearly reduce the environmental effectiveness of the ecotaxes. Programmes designed to assist polluters in abating pollution may weaken the incentive effects of environmental taxes. Moreover they may lead to an inefficiently high level of pollution abatement if the rate was already set to obtain the targeted level of environmental quality. In addition, if households and producers face different prices on some fossil fuels, this may lead to considerable incentives for tax evasion by consumers posing as producers and to considerable costs of tax evasion and of control intended to curb such tax evasion. Rebates or compensation schemes that help polluters cover pollution control costs may also reduce the effectiveness of the tax by reducing the possibility of withdrawal from the industry as a way of achieving environmental objectives. Moreover, compensation scheme reduce long-term social acceptance of the charge policy.

A crude approach to reducing both the loss in competitiveness and leakage is to exempt export-oriented industries, which would be most affected by an environmental tax, from having to pay the tax. Exemptions that are often designed to allow heavy polluters to remain competitive, within an industry or in the international arena, not only reduce the tax burden of the said industry, but they also make less energy-intensive industry comparatively disadvantaged. Moreover, rebates may mean that other groups end up facing a higher tax rate than the one that would be optimal in terms of efficiency if the environmental objective remains the same. It forces them to over-invest in pollution abatement and lowers the economic efficiency of the tax.

Border tax adjustments

Border tax adjustments (BTAs) involve the application to imports of domestic taxes and the remission of domestic taxes on exports of like products, and are used to neutralise the competitive effects of a domestic tax. Border tax adjustments raise three main questions. The first one involves the extent to which BTAs can further the environmental objectives of the environmental tax. The second question involves the legal question as to whether they would be allowed under international trade rules. The third main issue involves the practicability of imposing BTAs to compensate for taxes imposed on consumption and production patterns.

With regard to environmental effectiveness, border tax adjustments on products when pollution arises from consumption patterns can actually help make the environmental tax more efficient. However, policy makers should be aware that border tax adjustments may reduce

the effectiveness of environmental taxes, particularly in the case where pollution arises from production processes and methods. For instance, if the tax were to be somewhat imposed on imports and remitted on exports domestic consumption will fall, but producers in a small open economy can still sell their products at the world price, such that exports may increase and domestic pollution does not necessarily fall.

Overall, border tax adjustments can potentially neutralise the effects of an environmental tax on competitiveness. Such adjustments appear to pose no problems for the trading system when applied to products. However, they do when applied to processes and production methods (PPMs), because emissions taxes do not qualify for border tax adjustments. The rules for applying border tax adjustments to taxes on processes and process inputs need to be clarified. Even more important however, is the potential impact of BTAs on the effectiveness of environment taxes, particularly when applied to production processes and methods. Further research in this area is clearly needed. Moreover, the practical aspects or feasibility of applying border tax adjustments for taxes imposed on PPMs also need to be clarified. The issue of border tax adjustments is being addressed by the WTO Committee on Trade and Environment.

Another problem with border tax adjustments and global emissions, is that it may be intended to influence the behaviour of other countries to the advantage of the country imposing the ecotax. In most cases, the ecotax is designed based on the perspective of the domestic country only. Influencing foreign emissions, by influencing foreign output through the price mechanism would seem to be a very blunt instrument for achieving the aim of even the domestic country of reducing foreign emissions. This points to the desirability of basing policy in the case of an international externality on a cooperative, multilateral framework.

Implementation strategy

Implementation of environmental taxes should state clearly the objectives of the policy and where possible give a clear indication of the evolution of these taxes over time. The effect of the tax will depend not just on its current level but also on expectations about its future level, and on environmental policy in other countries. A clear distinction must be made between short term effects and longer term restructuring effects. Various options to redistribute the ecotax revenues could help reduce transitory costs. As discussed below, careful formulation of mitigation measures is necessary if one is to preserve the efficiency and effectiveness of the environmental policy, as they may prevent the necessary sectoral and technological restructuring in the economy from taking place. It is also important that both the domestic and international trade policy community be consulted before environmental taxes, which may have significant effects in trade, are implemented. Most importantly, in the case of international externalities, policies should be developed within a cooperative multilateral framework.

6.4. Distributive effects of environmental taxes and compensation measures

Many of OECD countries that have introduced environmental taxes have found that the distributional effects of these measures have been a major area of political controversy, and have required close attention in policy design and presentation. In fact, distributional issues matter for policy, both for "objective" and "pragmatic" reasons. In the first case, there may be policy objectives concerning the position of particular groups, such as the poor or the elderly, which concern policy-makers. In the second case, if the gains and losses from environmental tax policies are too unevenly distributed, the losers may form a powerful lobby opposing the introduction of environmental taxes.

Distributional issues may arise with environmental taxes to a greater extent than with other environmental policy instruments that do not give rise to revenues. Besides, environmental taxes are likely more visible than regulations. Although all environmental policies may involve distributional gainers and losers, environmental taxes raise the possibility that the burden of the tax payments may be unevenly distributed.

Baseline for comparison

What is meant by the distributional effects of environmental taxes will depend on what is taken as the baseline for comparison: that is the no-change baseline where no policy intervention takes place, or the baseline where some other instruments are used to achieve a similar environmental objective. In fact, various notions of distribution may be relevant, depending on the instruments being employed and the political context of policy making. These could include: the distributional effects across income groups, or other measures of relative households living standards; distribution among household types, especially among households according to age and household composition; distribution between business and households; distribution among types of firm, or across industries; and regional distribution.

Empirical evidence

There is a very limited empirical literature on the distributional effects of environmental taxes and possible compensating measures. In comparison with the extensive attention which has been paid to carbon and energy taxes, much less empirical evidence exists on the distributional effects of other possible environmental taxes, possibly because they relate to less significant components of household spending, with less of a clear-cut "necessity" status.

The case for mitigation and compensation measures

Ecotaxes can result in different cost and distributional impacts for various firms, sectors, regions and income groups, and offsetting measures may be necessary to ensure a greater acceptance of the tax and that other tax policy goals are met. In fact, governments may take mitigation measures to reduce *ex ante* the ecotax burden of those groups most likely to be affected by the tax. Environmental tax revenues may also be used to compensate *ex post* those most affected, either through regular or special compensation mechanisms. In any case, why should any greater case for compensation for the distributional effects of environmental taxes be made than for other policy measures and reforms? A readiness to make compensation to transitional losers from policy changes may expose governments to lobbying pressures. Besides, gains and losses from public policy changes may be small relative to the scale of gains and losses which arise from natural adjustment processes in the economy. Overall, equity objectives may be more efficiently achieved if an overall redistribution policy is designed, than if a distributional policy accumulates as a result of a sequence of *ad hoc* compensation measures for particular policy measures.

Moreover, compensation measures should not come in contradiction with the OECD polluter-pays-principle (PPP) which specifies that, as a general rule, Member countries should not assist the polluters in bearing the cost of pollution control by *e.g.* subsidies or tax advantages. Exceptions to this rule would be allowed for the transition period in which PPP is not yet fully implemented and only if all of the following conditions are met: *a)* if they are related to industries, areas or plants where severe difficulties would occur; *b)* if they were limited to well defined transition periods adapted to the specific socio-economic problems associated with the implementation of a country's environmental programme; and *c)* if they were not likely to create significant distortions in international trade and investment.

Distributional implications of tax reform: personal income

Given that people and not business entities end up bearing the final incidence of ecotaxes, governments may want to reduce other taxes that affect individuals. However, caution should be exercised so as not to exacerbate the regressivity of the environmental taxes. Policy-makers should be aware that such policies will not confer any benefit to non-taxpayers. In comparison to adjustments to income taxes, however, more benefit is likely to accrue to poorer households from reductions in sales taxes, since poor households may pay significant amounts of sales tax on their consumption, whilst being liable for little income tax. A reduction in sales tax rates on other necessities may also be considered but this would create many administrative difficulties and could create inefficiency in the tax system.

Targeting poorer households

It may be difficult to adequately compensate poorer households for the regressive burden of environmental taxes on energy by adjustments to the tax system alone. Poor households pay relatively little taxes, and using the tax system to return revenues to poor households will generally return much larger amounts of revenue to better-off households. It may be possible to target the return of revenues to poorer households through adjustments to public transfer systems, but any special adjustments might reduce the incentive to work since it will further reduce the gap between wages and social benefits. A more targeted approach to compensation, perhaps including reduced energy costs for the vulnerable elderly poor, or measures to improve the energy efficiency of their homes, may be required.

Market failures

Environmental taxes give rise to two adjustment costs: the additional tax payments, and the impact of the tax on output. Both of these costs may be greater if energy consumers are prevented by market failures from making optimal adjustments in energy use. Market failures may include credit market failures, informational failures, and certain market failures related to housing tenure. Where households are prevented by market failures from adjusting efficiently to higher energy prices, their reductions in energy consumption in response to higher energy prices will tend to be smaller, and more "painful" in terms of their welfare cost. The social and distributional costs of higher energy prices may be exacerbated if market failures in energy efficiency investment are particularly concentrated amongst low income households, or other vulnerable groups. Measures to rectify the underlying market failures would then have the twin merits that they would tend to reduce the aggregate economic cost of achieving a given reduction in consumption, and at the same time would also help to reduce the social and distributional cost of higher energy taxation.

6.5. The use of environmental tax revenues

Options for revenue recycling

In general, the degree of acceptance of any new tax will be partly related to what the authorities intend to use the revenues for, and if some form of compensation measures is planned. It is often in this context that the issue of environmental tax reform is raised. Some advocate that the ecotax revenues should be earmarked and used entirely to finance environmental expenditures, some being specifically targeted to a particular pollution problem or particular groups. Others argue that the revenues should be part of total public revenues, and thereby part of the general spending programme and budgetary process. In this case, some suggest that the revenues should be used to reduce government deficits, and others argue

that the revenues should be used to reduce other taxes. Yet, others argue that the revenues should be used to offer some form of compensation to those mostly affected by the tax in a way that would not reduce the incentive effects of the tax. The degree of importance of these issues will depend on the relative importance of the tax base in the economy and of the ecotax revenues in government budgets, and on whether the tax aims at the reduction or complete elimination of the polluting products. In any case, the use of ecotax revenues should be determined in a context of opportunity costs, where the revenues may be used not only for environmental purposes, but also for other social and economic reasons. As the social, environmental and economic circumstances will vary over time, so may the preferred option for the use of revenues.

The decision to recycle the revenues will depend on the circumstances of the country concerned. That is on the size of the budget deficit and the tax burden, the functioning of capital and labour markets, consumption patterns, the design of the tax system and the country's natural endowments. The availability of revenues, particularly from levies such as energy taxes which could raise substantial sums, is not an argument in itself for introducing a new tax. The argument for introducing the tax should primarily rest on the environmental objectives. Nevertheless, the revenues could offer a means of buying political acceptability.

As observed earlier, there will be pressure to compensate consumers and producers who are particularly affected by the new tax, and this will reduce the revenues available for tax reform or for reducing the deficit.

Employment and environmental policy integration

Governments should in principle adopt those environmental policy instruments that reach maximum environmental effects with lowest economic impact. Labour market rigidities may imply in some countries that any revenues available would be best used to cut taxes on labour, such as social security contributions. Such a tax shift has been widely proposed as a way of delivering a "double dividend" of a cleaner environment and increased employment. The existence and size of any double dividend depends on the effectiveness of labour tax cuts in increasing employment and on how much of the burden of the environmental tax is borne by labour. Overall, the employment effects are difficult to determine and will vary significantly between countries, but available evidence suggests the employment impact of a tax shift of this type is likely to be small in the long term.

Optimal use of revenues: a separate issue

A cost efficient policy would be the best policy for employment purposes, and this is why environmental taxes are advocated instead of command and control. Moreover, the careful use of the ecotax revenues may be used to offset some of the costs associated with environmental taxes. In any case, environmental taxes should be used first and foremost for environmental purposes, and the use of revenues should be based on budgetary, fiscal and economic criteria.

The desirability of different uses of energy tax revenues will vary with the circumstances of the country introducing the tax. Like any other tax, an energy tax will face political and economic resistance, in the form of pressure for compensation in the form of higher transfer payments, higher wages and industrial assistance. The revenues from the energy tax provide an opportunity for offsetting the cost of pollution abatement, but do not themselves provide a rationale for introducing a new tax: the argument rests primarily on the environmental benefits.

ANNEXES

ENVIRONMENTAL TAXATION OF ENERGY

Systematic taxation of fuels according to their environmental characteristics is a comparatively recent idea, and whilst carbon taxes or other environmental taxes on energy sources have been discussed in many countries, only a few countries have so far implemented any systematic energy tax structure along environmental lines. In fact, five European countries have implemented carbon taxes: Denmark, Finland, the Netherlands, Norway and Sweden. The annex gives an overview of the tax burden of energy products in these countries. A more detailed description of the structure and administration of these carbon taxes may be found after this overview.

Overall, the tax reforms in the energy sectors of those five countries have effectively raised the share of all taxes included in end-user prices of fossil fuels for households. Here, taxes include energy excise taxes, carbon taxes, SO_2 and NO_X taxes, as well as the value of VAT (see Table A.1). To the exception of Denmark and Norway, taxes in per cent of end-user prices of leaded gasoline have increased by more than 11 percentage points. The share of taxes of premium unleaded gasoline has risen in all five countries, particularly in Finland. Diesel is the fuel that has had the greatest increase, particularly in Denmark, Norway and Sweden. The share of taxes in light fuel oil prices has increased in all countries. In Sweden, it has increased by more than 10 percentage points, and in Finland by more than 7 percentage points.

The next three charts present end-user prices and taxes paid for leaded, unleaded and diesel, for the countries where the fuel is available and for those countries that the data on prices and taxes existed for the two years 1990 and 1994. The percentages represent the share of taxes in end-user prices. Prices and taxes are converted to US dollars using Purchasing Power Parities to account for difference in the cost of living in each country. Prices and taxes paid on diesel are those paid by industry, and are exclusive of Value Added Taxes.

One direct observation is that end-user prices and the tax burden greatly vary across OECD countries. Differences in prices are in part explained by differences in tax burden, but also by other factors such as adequate infrastructure for the transport of fossil fuels. Prices of unleaded have generally increased since 1990, and rising tax burdens appear to be the major reason for those rising prices. Countries that have introduced CO_2 taxes, like Finland and Norway have had large increases in prices, as well as in tax burden, but other countries like Germany, Greece and the United Kingdom have had a more than proportional increase in tax burden.

Table A.1. **Percentage of Taxes in End-User Fuel Prices for Households**

	Leaded gasoline	Premium unleaded	Diesel	Light fuel oil
Denmark				
1990	69.1	62.4	18.0	62.0
1991	67.8	60.3	35.2	60.1
1992	67.2	61.7	51.7	63.6
1993	64.6	60.4	52.2	62.7
1994	68.0	64.5	53.2	64.0
Finland				
1990	55.2	51.4	58.7	20.4
1991	61.2	57.7	60.4	21.1
1992	68.0	64.3	62.0	21.4
1993	71.8	69.7	63.0	24.6
1994	n.a.	71.8	69.1	27.9
Netherlands				
1990	64.5	62.4	52.2	33.4
1991	68.1	65.8	54.3	33.3
1992	72.4	69.8	57.4	36.3
1993	72.5	70.2	61.0	38.8
1994	75.9	74.6	65.7	n.a.
Norway				
1990	62.5	60.8	29.3	31.1
1991	68.1	65.1	36.9	39.5
1992	71.6	68.5	35.5	38.0
1993	72.1	69.1	43.5	33.8
1994	67.3	71.3	55.7	33.9
Sweden				
1990	65.5	n.a.	41.4	47.0
1991	67.7	n.a.	44.3	55.2
1992	69.2	n.a.	45.9	58.9
1993	74.7	70.6	45.4	54.2
1994	76.5	72.2	58.6	57.5

Source: Based on IEA Quarterly "Energy Prices and taxes".

Leaded gasoline is usually more expensive than unleaded gasoline, and the tax differential between leaded and unleaded gasoline would appear as the major factor. With the exception of Denmark and Portugal, the price of leaded gasoline has increased in all countries from 1990 to 1994. Leaded gasoline is no longer sold in Austria, Canada, Japan and The United States.

The price of diesel has also increased in most countries, except Austria, New Zealand, Portugal, Turkey and the United States.

Annex 1 Figure 1. **Prices and taxes on unleaded gasoline:** (95 Ron) sold to households (including VAT) in US Purchasing Power Parities per litre

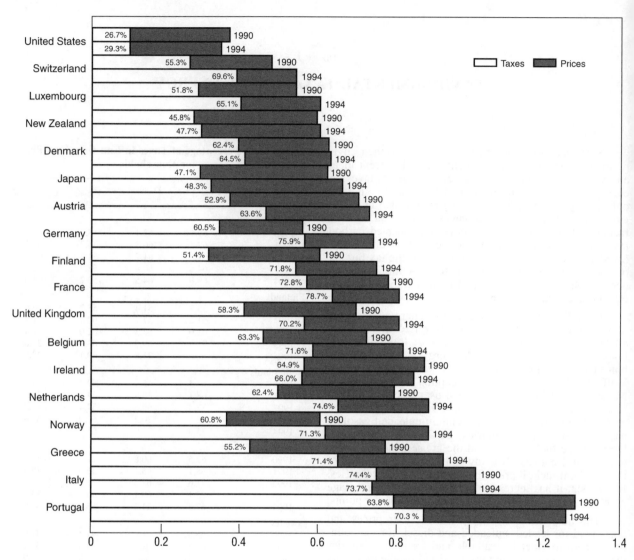

Source: Based on IEA Quarterly Report "Energy Prices and Taxes: Fourth Quarter 1994".

Annex 1 Figure 2. **Prices and taxes on leaded gasoline:**
sold to households (including VAT) in US Purchasing Power Parities per litre

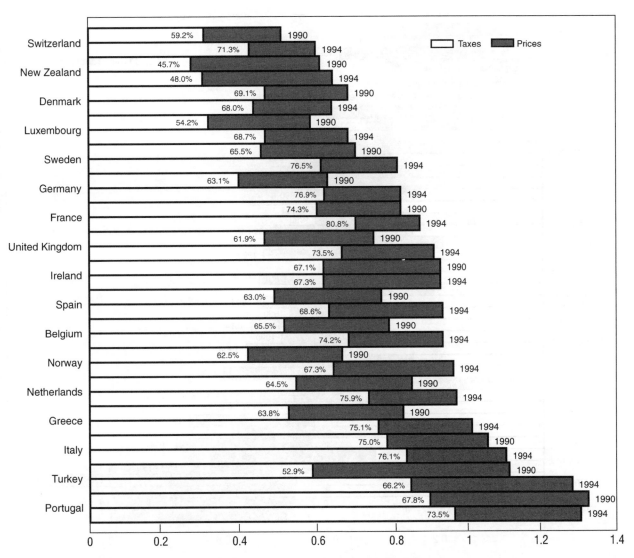

Source: Based on IEA Quarterly Report "Energy Prices and Taxes: fourth quarter 1994".

Annex 1 Figure 3. **Effective prices and taxes on diesel**
used by Industry in US Purchasing Power Parities per litre (excluding VAT)

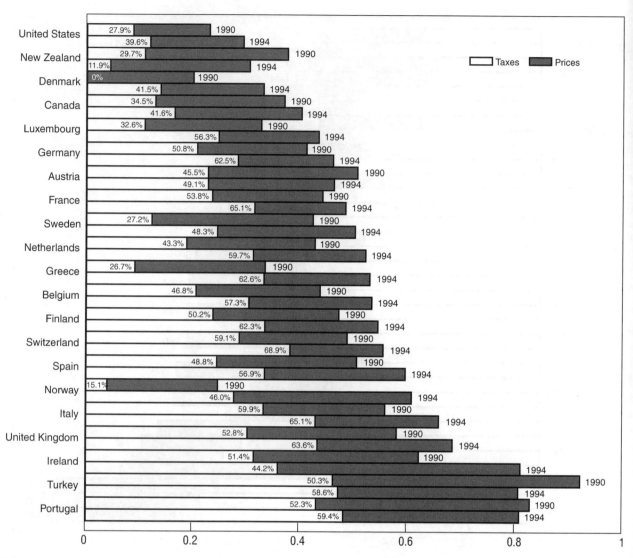

Source: Based on IEA Quarterly Report "Energy Prices and Taxes: Fourth Quarter 1994".

ENVIRONMENTAL TAXES IN ENERGY SECTORS

As noted in previous sections, five countries have implemented carbon taxes: Denmark, Finland, the Netherlands, Norway and Sweden. What follows is more detailed information on the structure and administration of these carbon taxes. The tables describe the various excise taxes that were imposed on energy products over the last three years.

Denmark

In Denmark, a carbon dioxide tax was first introduced in 1992 as part of a tax package, which comprised eight laws which included a CO_2 tax on energy consumption and various subsidy schemes for promoting means to produce electricity and heat from less carbon-rich fuels such as natural gas and biofuels, and to increase energy efficiency. The CO_2 tax was imposed on all types of CO_2 emissions sources in Denmark except gasoline, natural gas and biofuels, and was based on the CO_2 content of each fuel at combustion. The overall rate was 100 DKr per tonne CO_2. In 1993, the total net revenue of the CO_2 tax was DKr 3 174 million.

Generally, 50 per cent of the CO_2 tax was reimbursed to businesses registered under the VAT law, except the CO_2 tax on diesel used for motor fuels which could not be reimbursed. Further reimbursement for the other 50 per cent was possible: 50 per cent of the tax that exceeded 1 per cent of the refund base, 75 per cent of the tax beyond 2 per cent of the refund base and 90 per cent of the tax beyond 3 per cent of the refund base could be reimbursed. The refund base is the difference between the total sales liable to VAT including exports and the total purchase liable to VAT including imports. If the CO_2 tax was beyond 3 per cent of the refund base and if the company had been subject to an energy audit, a subsidy was granted corresponding to the part of the CO_2 tax that had not been reimbursed according to the above mentioned rules. However, companies always had to pay DKr 10 000 per year. This arrangement was made to compensate businesses that rely heavily on energy in their production processes. The carbon tax was not reimbursed to households.

Aviation, shipping and gas consumption on refineries were exempted from CO_2 charges. It was considered most appropriate to impose CO_2 tax on electricity at the final consumption and to calculate the tax according to the CO_2 content in coal based electricity. With a view to support or compensate the CO_2-free or CO_2-low production of electricity, a special law was passed according to which a subsidy of DKr 0.10 per kWh could be given to producers of electricity for the quantity of electricity produced by renewable energy and renewable fuels or by decentralised heat and power generation based on natural gas. Furthermore, a subsidy of DKr 0.17 per kWh was granted on electricity produced by wind power, water power, biogas and biofuels.

Before the introduction of the CO_2 tax, there were already excise duties imposed on energy products. Leaded and unleaded gasoline have been imposed at different rates since the mid-1980s. The market share of unleaded gasoline is now nearly 100 per cent. Besides excise duties, consumers of fuels and energy products had to pay Value Added Tax at a rate of 25 per cent. The following table compares the rates of the excise duty and the CO_2 tax for 1993 and 1994.

Tax Rates on Fuels and Electricity: Denmark

Energy source	Unit	Excise Tax		Carbon Tax	
		1993	1994	1993	1994
Unleaded Petrol[a]	DKr/litre	2.25	2.45	–	–
Leaded Petrol[a]	DKr/litre	2.90	3.10	–	–
Diesel Oil, light	DKr/litre	1.67	1.67	0.27[b]	0.27[b]
Diesel Oil, ordinary	DKr/litre	1.77	1.77	0.27[b]	0.27[b]
Light Fuel Oil	DKr/litre	1.49[c]	1.49[c]	0.27[d]	0.27[d]
Heavy Fuel Oil	DKr/kg	1.66[c]	1.66[c]	0.32[d]	0.32[d]
Fuel tar	DKr/kg	1.50	1.50	0.28	0.28
Kerosine, heating	DKr/litre	1.49	1.49	0.27	0.27
Kerosine	DKr/litre	1.77	1.77	0.27	0.27
Coal	DKr/tonne	690[c]	690[c]	242[d]	242[d]
Petroleum Coke	DKr/tonne	690	690	323	323
Lignite	DKr/tonne	505	505	178	178
Gas used as motor fuel	DKr/litre	1.18	1.18	0.16	0.16
Other Gas (LPG)	DKr/kg	2.00	2.00	0.30	0.30
Refinery gas	DKr/kg	2.00	2.00	0.29	0.29
Electricity	DKr/kWh	0.27	0.30	0.10	0.10
Electricity, heating	DKr/kWh	0.24	0.27	0.10	0.10

a) An Environmental Pool tax on gasoline has been levied since 1.4.1993 at 0.025 DKr/litre and was increased to 0.04 DKr/litre.
b) The CO_2 tax is not refundable to industrial consumers.
c) The excise tax on LFO/HFO and coal is refundable to industry.
d) The carbon tax on LFO/HFO and coal is only 50% refundable to industry.
Source: OECD.

The 1994 tax reform increased the excise tax rates on electricity, motor fuels and coal, but did not affect the CO_2 tax rates. The next table shows the total charges imposed before and after the tax reform, that is in 1993 and in 1994. The tax reform will be fully implemented in 1998. The tax rates shown are VAT-inclusive (25 per cent).

The charge on gasoline increased by DKr 0.20/litre in 1994, and will increase gradually until 1998. The increase in the tax on diesel will take place in the years 1995 to 1997, and will be DKr 0.35/litre in 1997. The charge on electricity is to increase by DKr 0.19 to DKr 0.46 from 1994 to 1998. On top of that the consumer will pay the CO_2 tax of DKr 0.10 each year.

Total Charge Rate on Fuels: Denmark
Inclusive of VAT

Fuels	Unit	1993	1994	1995	1996	1997	1998
Gasoline, leaded	DKr/litre	3.63	3.88	4.44	4.66	4.73	4.79
Gasoline, unleaded	DKr/litre	2.81	3.06	3.63	3.85	3.91	3.98
Diesel, ordinary	DKr/litre	2.55	2.55	2.84	2.86	2.99	2.99
of which: CO_2 tax	DKr/litre	0.34	0.34	0.34	0.34	0.34	0.34
Diesel, light	DKr/litre	2.43	2.43	2.71	2.74	2.86	2.86
of which: CO_2 tax	DKr/litre	0.34	0.34	0.34	0.34	0.34	0.34
Auto gas	DKr/litre	1.68	1.68	1.88	2.04	2.13	2.13
Electricity	DKr/kWh	0.46	0.50	0.54	0.58	0.63	0.70
of which: CO_2 tax	DKr/kWh	0.13	0.13	0.13	0.13	0.13	0.13
Electricity, heating	DKr/kWh	0.42	0.46	0.49	0.53	0.58	0.62
of which: CO_2 tax	DKr/kWh	0.13	0.13	0.13	0.13	0.13	0.13
Coal	DKr/tonne	1165	1165	1265	1378	1490	1603
of which: CO_2 tax	DKr/tonne	303	303	303	303	303	303

Source: OECD.

Finland

In January 1990, Finland introduced Europe's first explicit carbon tax, imposed on fossil fuels according to their carbon content. This carbon tax was initially set at the comparatively low level of Mk 24.5 per ton of carbon. The carbon tax was incorporated – as a surtax – into the excise duty on fossil fuels. In 1993, the tax rate was doubled to Mk 50, and a new mode of tax differentiation was introduced for diesel oil and petrol.

The excise duty on fuels was restructured as of January 1994, and the tax rates were raised. At present, the tax is split into a "fiscal" component with tax differentiations for diesel and petrol, and a "carbon/energy" component (which replaced the pure carbon component). The relative weights of the carbon content and the energy content are 60/40 in terms of total revenues. The tax rates are raised again for 1995: the carbon rate was set at Mk 141 per ton of carbon (Mk 38.3 per ton of CO_2) and the energy rate at Mk 3.5 per MWh. The excise tax rates as from 1 January 1995, and for 1993 and 1994 are as follows:

Tax Rates on Fuels and Electricity: Finland

Fuels	Unit tax	Basic tax			Energy/CO_2		
		1993	1994	1995	1993[f]	1994	1995
Unleaded Petrol[a, c]	Mk/litre	2.35	2.36	2.61	0.05	0.071	0.123
Leaded Petrol[a, c]	Mk/litre	2.35	2.81	3.06	0.50	0.071	0.123
Diesel Oil[b, c]	Mk/litre	0.87	1.65	1.65	0.27	0.078	0.135
Light Fuel Oil[c]	Mk/litre	0.042	0.042	0.0428	0.0417	0.08	0.137
Heavy Fuel Oil[c]	Mk/kg	0.025	0.025	0.0255	0.0417	0.093	0.160
Coal	Mk/tonne	–	–	–	33.38	67.2	116.1
Peat[d]	Mk/MWh	–	–	–	4.17	4.3	3.5
Natural Gas[e]	Mk/nm^3	–	–	–	0.0209	0.065	0.112
Electricity							
Nuclear	Mk/kWh	0.015	0.015	0.015	0.0062	0.0062	0.009
Hydro	Mk/kWh	0.015	–	–	–	0.002	0.004
Imported	Mk/kWh	0.015	0.007	0.013	0.0062	0.0062	0.009

a) Basic Tax 0.05 Mk/litre lower for reformulated petrol.
b) Basic Tax 0.15 Mk/litre lower for sulphur-free diesel.
c) Additional Precautionary stock feeds are imposed on liquid fuels.
d) Peat is exempt from carbon component.
e) Only 50% of the rate is applied to natural gas in 1995.
f) Before the introduction of the Energy/CO_2 tax in 1994, there was an Environmental Damage Tax.
Source: OECD.

Exemptions or reduced rates are not applied for industries. Products used as raw materials in industrial production, or used as fuels for planes and certain vessels are exempted from the tax. Estimated total revenues for 1995 from the basic tax on energy products amount to Mk 10 200 million and to 2 400 million from the additional energy/CO_2 tax, and for 1994, to Mk 8 800 million and Mk 1 450 million respectively.

The Netherlands

When it was introduced in 1988, the environmental charge on fuels replaced a system of programme specific levies, raising revenue for specific types of environmental expenditure. The environmental charge on fuels was developed in response to a perceived need for an integral system for financing environmental policy expenditures. Fuel was chosen as the tax base, because it was felt that this would provide a "general" link with the polluter-pays-principle. Many pollution problems are directly related to fuel usage. Furthermore, fuel use was considered to be a rough indicator for economic activities resulting in pollution.

Since 1988, the tax base has been changed considerably over the years. In 1990, a CO_2-component was added to the tax base, providing Gld 150 million of extra revenue. Refinery gas was added to the tax base in 1991. The earmarking received various criticisms, and since July 1992 revenues are for the general budget, with the Minister of Finance being primarily responsible. In 1992, the entire tax base was changed to one based 50/50 on energy/carbon content. The next table gives the tax rates on different types of fuels, derived from their energy and carbon content applicable on 1 January 1993, 1994 and 1995. In addition to excise duties and the environmental tax, there is also a compulsory storage charge imposed at Gld 0.0135 per litre on leaded and unleaded gasoline diesel and light fuel oil. The revenues from the environmental tax for 1995 are expected to amount to Gld 1 400 million or about 1.3 per cent of total tax revenue.

Tax Rates on Fuels: Netherlands

Fuels	Unit	Excise Duties			Environmental tax		
		1993	1994	1995	1993	1994	1995
Unleaded Petrol	Gld/litre	0.9715	1.0815	1.082	0.0241	0.0241	0.0251
Leaded Petrol	Gld/litre	1.093	1.2193	1.2193	0.0241	0.0241	0.0251
Diesel Oil	Gld/litre	0.5552	0.6352	0.6352	0.0266	0.0266	0.0277
Light Fuel Oil	Gld/litre	0.1026	0.1026	0.1023	0.0265	0.0265	0.0275
Heavy Fuel Oil	Gld/tonne	34.24	34.24	34.24	31.04	31.04	32.33
LPG	Gld/tonne	–	78.72	78.72	31.83	31.83	33.08
Coal	Gld/tonne	–	–	–	22.64	22.64	23.38
Blast Furnace, cokes oven, refinery and coal gas	Gld/1 000 GJ	–	–	–	220.57	220.57	236.82
Natural Gas							
0-10 mn m^3	Gld/1 000 GJ	–	–		20.79	20.79	21.55
> 10 mn m^3	Gld/1 000 GJ	–			13.67	13.67	14.10
Residuals (traded)							
Petrocokes	Gld/tonne	–	–	–	31.03	31.03	32.47
Liquid	Gld/tonne	–	–	–	31.04	31.04	32.33
Gaseous	Gld/1 000 GJ	–	–	–	220.57	220.57	236.82

Source: OECD.

Norway

In Norway, the current tax system for fossil fuels already includes taxes on atmospheric emissions of CO_2, SO_2 and lead, in addition to the general Value Added Tax of 23 per cent. Both the petrol and mineral oil tax contain a CO_2 element. A carbon tax has also been introduced for gas and oil combustion on the continental shelf and as from 1 July 1992, a carbon tax was introduced for certain coal and coke applications. Moreover, the petrol tax has been differentiated based on lead content and the mineral oil tax based on sulphur content.

CO_2 taxes were introduced on 1 January 1991, starting at a rate of NKr 0.60/litre which was increased to NKr 0.80/litre on 1 January 1992, to NKr 0.82 on 1 January 1994 and then to NKr 0.83 on 1 January 1995. Besides its environmental importance, the CO_2 tax represents an important element of the national budget. In 1994, the tax on CO_2 gave state revenues of about 6 billion NKr.

Petrol also faces a basic tax which was on 1 January 1994 NKr 3.78/litre of leaded gasoline and NKr 3.12/litre of unleaded gasoline. The basic tax on petrol differentiates leaded petrol and unleaded petrol since 1986. The lead surcharge since 1990 was increased many times from 0.43 NKr/l on 1 January 1990, to 0.53 on 1 January 1991, to 0.65 NKr/litre on 1 January 1992 and to 0.66 NKr/litre on 1 January 1994. Since 1995, the rate is also differentiated for leaded petrol: below 0.05 g of lead per litre of petrol the rate is NKr 3.79, and above 0.05 g of lead per litre the rate is NKr 4.24.

The SO_2 tax is levied on light and heavy fuel oil and is calculated on each 0.25 per cent of sulphur content and per litre. Oil with lower sulphur content than 0.05 per cent is exempted. The tax rate is 0.07 NKr per litre light fuel oil and 0.63 NKr per litre of heavy fuel oil and has remained unchanged since 1 January 1991.

The next table gives the tax rates on different types of fuels, derived from their energy and carbon content applicable in Norway in 1 January 1993 and 1994.

Tax Rates on Fuels and Electricity: Norway

Fuels	Unit	Excise Duties			CO$_2$ Tax			SO$_2$ Tax		
		1993	1994	1995	1993	1994	1995	1993	1994	1995
Unleaded Petrol	NKr/litre	3.07	3.12	3.57	0.80	0.82	0.83	–	–	–
Leaded Petrol	NKr/litre	3.72	3.78	4.24[a]	0.80	0.82	0.83	–	–	–
Diesel Oil	NKr/litre	2.45[b]	2.45	2.87	0.40	0.41	0.415	0.07	0.07	0.07
Light Fuel Oil	NKr/litre	0	–	–	0.40	0.41	0.415	0.07	0.07	0.07
Heavy Fuel Oil[c]	NKr/litre	6	–	–	0.40	0.41	0.415	0.63	0.63	0.63
Coal	NKr/kg	–	–	–	0.40	0.41	0.415	–	–	–
Natural Gas[d]		–	–	–	–	–	–	–	–	–
Electricity										
Consumption	NKr/kWh	0.046	0.051	0.052	–	–	–	–	–	–
Production	Nkr/kWh	0.012	0.0122	0.0152	–	–	–	–	–	–

a) The rate for leaded gasoline with less than 0.05 g of lead per litre is NKr 3.79, and above 0.05 g/litre the rate is NKr 4.24/litre.
b) As of 1 October 1993.
c) The sulphur tax is for each 0.25% content of sulphur. However, the tax is rebated if the sulphur content is removed before its end-use. Since 1 January 1992, oil with a sulphur content lower than 0.05 per cent is exempted.
d) No consumption of natural gas.
Source: OECD.

Sweden

The Swedish tax reform of 1990 and 1991 introduced VAT on all kinds of energy consumption, except fuels used by aeroplanes. The present tax rate is 25 per cent. The reform also included a new system of energy taxation to take account of various forms of polluting emissions. A carbon tax on fossil fuels equivalent to SEK 0.25 per kg of carbon dioxide emitted was introduced on 1 January 1991. This tax was also imposed on fuel used in certain domestic air traffic. A sulphur tax was also introduced in 1991. To limit the overall tax burden on energy due to new environmental taxes, the energy tax on fossil fuel and electricity was reduced.

Sweden introduced a new energy and carbon tax system in the beginning of 1993. The carbon dioxide tax for the manufacturing industry and commercial horticulture was reduced to 25 per cent of the general level. At the same time, the energy tax on fuels and electricity was abolished for the manufacturing industry and commercial horticulture. Further tax reductions can be applicable to enterprises with a very high consumption of energy – such as cement and lime manufacturing. The revenue effect was balanced by an increase of the general level of the carbon dioxide tax (from 0.25 to SEK 0.32 per kg CO$_2$), as well as an increase of energy tax on electricity used by non-industrial consumers. The reduced rates for manufacturing industry and commercial horticulture do not apply on fuels used as propellant in cars, buses and lorries, *e.g.* petrol and diesel.

Petrol, gas oil, heavy fuel oil, kerosene, LPG, methane, natural gas, coal and petroleum coke are directly subject to energy tax, carbon dioxide and sulphur tax.

The sulphur tax is also levied on peat. The general principle is that excise duties are only to be paid if the fuel is used as motor fuel or for heating purposes. Apart from fuels directly taxable, excise duties are also levied to any product used as motor fuel and to any liquid or gaseous hydrocarbon which is sold or used for heating purposes.

The energy and carbon tax rates for 1995 are presented in the table below. The carbon tax rate for 1995 correspond to SEK 0.34 per kg of CO$_2$ emitted. The environmental tax on domestic air traffic is levied at a rate of SEK 1 per kg of fuel consumed plus SEK 12 per kg of hydrocarbon and nitrogen oxides assumed to be emitted. Tax rates on sulphur content amount for coal, petroleum coke and peat to SEK 30 per kg SO$_2$ and liquid fuels – such as diesel oils and heating oils – to SEK 27 per m^3 and 0.1 per cent by weight of the sulphur content. However, oil products with a sulphur content of a maximum of 0.1 per cent by weight is exempted from tax. If sulphur control measures are applied, the tax is rebated with SEK 30 per kg reduced sulphur emitted.

Exemption from energy tax, carbon dioxide tax and sulphur tax is granted for: fuels used for other purposes than as motor fuels or as heating fuels; coal and petroleum coke used in metallurgical processes, fuels used by railway locomotives, aeroplanes or ships. Furthermore fuels used for producing electricity are exempted from energy tax and carbon dioxide tax (not from sulphur tax).

The total revenue from energy tax and carbon dioxide tax on fossil fuels and electricity for the fiscal year 1993/94 amounted to SEK 38.7 billion (the carbon dioxide tax raised 11.3 billion). The revenue from the sulphur tax for the same period was SEK 230 million.

From the start of 1992 a direct charge of SEK 40 per kg of nitrogen oxide emissions was levied from large furnaces with an annual production of at least 50 gWh. The revenues are to be redistributed to the furnaces on the basis of the amount of energy produced. As from 1996, the charge system will gradually apply to smaller plants with an energy production of 25-50 gWh per year. The extension is to be made in two steps. The first step is to be taken on 1 January 1996 when the charge threshold will be lowered from 50 gWh to 40 gWh. Finally on 1 January 1997 the threshold will be reduced to 25 gWh.

Tax Rates on Fuels and Electricity: Sweden [a, b]

Fuels	Unit	Energy Tax			Carbon dioxide Tax		
		1993	1994	1995	1993	1994	1995
Unleaded Petrol [c]	SKr/litre	3.14	3.14	3.22	0.74	0.77	0.79
Leaded Petrol	SKr/litre	3.65	3.65	3.81	0.74	0.77	0.79
Diesel Oil [d, e] used as propellant							
Class 1	SKr/litre	1.31	1.31 (1.41)	1.42	0.92	0.96	0.98
Class 2	SKr/litre	1.59	1.60	1.64	0.92	0.96	0.98
Class 3	SKr/litre	1.84	1.86	1.91	0.92	0.96	0.98
Light and Heavy Fuel Oil [e]	SKr/m³	540	562	577	920	957	982
Coal	SKr/tonne	230	239	245	800	832	854
Natural Gas [f]	SKr/1 000 m³	175	182	187	680	707	725
LPG [g]	SKr/tonne	105	109	112	960	998	1024
Consumption tax on Electricity [h]	SKr/kWh	8.5	8.8	9.0	0	0	0
Biomass	SKr/tonne	0	0	0	0	0	0
Biofuels [i]							
Pure ethanol and vegetable oils	SKr/litre	0	0	0	0	0	0
Ethanol and methanol used in mixtures with other fuel components	SKr/litre	0.80	0.80	0.82	0	0	0

a) The excise rates do not include the sulphur tax. The average sulphur tax content in coal and heavy fuel oil are estimated to be 0.5 per cent by weight. For peat, the estimation is 0.24 per cent by weight.

b) Sweden applies reduced excise rates on fuels and electricity consumed by manufacturing industry. No energy tax is paid on such consumption, but only 25% of the carbon dioxide tax. The reduced tax rates do not apply to fuels used for propulsion of cars, lorries and buses.

c) As from 1 December 1994, Sweden applies a differentiated energy tax on unleaded petrol based on the environmental quality of the products (based on the sulphur-, lead-, benzene-, and phosphorous contents and vapour pressure). The tax rate for Class 2 is SKr 3.14 per litre (in 1995 3.22/litre) and for Class 3 SKr 3.20 per litre (1995 3.28 per litre) Class 1 is reserved for future more environmental friendly petrol.

d) As of 1 October 1993, the mileage tax is replaced by a special tax on diesel oil used as a propellant. The mileage tax was based on the type of vehicle and the weight of the vehicle. The special tax on diesel is included in the energy tax presented.

e) From 1 January 1991 until 1 July 1994 three different rates of energy tax applied on oil products based on the environmental quality of the products. As from 1 July 1994 the differentiation has been shifted from the energy tax to an equal differentiation of the special tax on diesel. On 1 July 1994 the diesel tax on Class 1 fuel was increased by SKr 0.1 per litre.

f) As from 1 January 1995, natural gas used as a propellant is taxed with an energy tax of SKr 1 498/1 000 m³.

g) On LPG used as a propellant the following taxes are levied (energy tax = E, CO_2-tax = C):
In 1993 E = SKr 0.85/litre, C = 0.48/litre.
In 1994 E = 0.88/litre and C = 0.50/litre.
In 1995 E = 0.90/litre and C = 0.51/litre.

h) Reduced rates applies when consumed for electricity-, gas-, water-, or heating supplies and when consumed in certain areas, mainly in the northern parts of Sweden. Electricity consumed by manufacturing industry are exempt. There are also two additional taxes on electricity which apply to the production of electricity in nuclear plants (SKr 0.002 per kWh) and power stations built before 1977 (SKr 0.02 if built before 1973 and SKr 0.01 if built between 1973 and 1977). These taxes are paid by the producer and are not refunded to the manufacturing industry.

i) As from 1 January 1995, biofuels are taxed with the same rates as diesel or petrol. But the government allows the above listed reduced excise rates for ethanol, methanol and vegetable oils used in pilot projects.

Source: OECD.